Fiscal Harmonization in the European Communities

National Politics and International Cooperation

Donald J. Puchala
Institute of International Studies
University of South Carolina

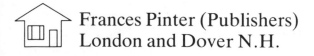
Frances Pinter (Publishers)
London and Dover N.H.

© Donald J. Puchala 1984

First published in Great Britain in 1984 by
Frances Pinter (Publishers) Limited
5 Dryden Street, London WC2E 9NW

Published in the United States of America in 1984 by
Frances Pinter (Publishers), 51 Washington Street,
Dover, New Hampshire

British Library Cataloguing in Publication Data

Puchala, Donald J.
    Fiscal harmonization in the European Communities.
    1. Finance, Public—European Economic
    Community countries
    I. Title
    336'.012'4   HJ1000.5
    ISBN 0-86187-465-X

Library of Congress Catalog No. 84-42764

Typeset by Joshua Associates, Oxford
Printed by SRP, Ltd., Exeter, Great Britain

To
Jeanne, Susan, Elizabeth and Madeline

Contents

Preface

Some twelve years ago, when the research for this book began, the European Communities were thriving. Trade was expanding and economies were growing rapidly. The institutions of the Common Market were functioning reasonably effectively, their legitimacy was increasing and their efforts to push Europeans toward thinking and acting in an environment beyond the nation-state were modestly succeeding. Steps were afoot to expand the Community's agenda for collective action into issue areas that were not strictly economic. 'Europe's' membership was expanding. Contemporary analysts hailed Europe in the early 1970s as a 'superpower in the making,' a new civilian 'third force' in world affairs and a crucial pole in an emergent trilateral world.

During this promising era in European integration prevailing academic interests were fixed on questions of evolution. Dozens of books and scores of articles pondered and predicted Europe's economic and political destiny. When would a United States of Europe finally emerge? Elaborate theories were put forth to explain the apparent transformation of a system of sovereign states into a federation, and mathematical formulas were derived to depict the pattern of integration and predict its future course.

But while analytic attention during the last heyday of European integration was being attracted to questions about what Europe might become, other questions about what Europe in the late 1960s and early 1970s actually *was* were slighted. What this Europe of the maturing EEC was, and indeed what it probably remains even with its current difficulties, is a cluster of governments and a community of peoples who have shown themselves able to engage in peaceful, transnational problem-solving concerning a broadening range of issues over an extended period of time. Attaining such an ability is a notable accomplishment that is both rare in the history of international relations and remarkable in the history of Europe. In this sense, the essence of what many have been calling 'European Integration' is not supranational amalgamation, of which there has been little, but rather continuing international cooperation, of which there has been a good deal. Consequently, understanding why and how the governments and peoples of the European Communities have been able to cooperate so productively for so long must be at least as important as speculating about whether they will fully unite at some time in the future.

This book then is about international cooperation. Its substantive focus is on the European Communities of the sixties and seventies because that is where some rather impressive international cooperation was taking place. The subject of the book is fiscal harmonization in the European Communities because issues concerning common taxes in the Common Market challenged member countries' capacities to cooperate. Examining how these issues were resolved reveals something of the political dynamics of international cooperation. The study's thesis is that successful international cooperation requires high degrees of mutual sensitivity on the part of interacting governments, particularly regarding one another's domestic politics. We all know this, of course. But how frequently do governments actually display such sensitivities? In the 1960s and 1970s EEC governments did, and that is why they were able to formulate and implement common policies. The book shows this.

Whether the governments of the EEC are still able to cooperate in the way they did a decade ago was not the immediate concern of this study. The research focused on the past. It led, however, to some conclusions about the conditions for successful international cooperation among democratic countries. Progress toward greater European Integration in the 1980s will depend upon the extent to which the governments and peoples of the European Communities can preserve those conditions for cooperation that remain and recreate those that disappeared in the economic and political turbulence of recent years.

This book has been in the making for a number of years. Three of the four national case studies of fiscal harmonization that constitute the substantive chapters of the study were previously published in abbreviated form, and Chapter 2's chronological overview also appeared before, albeit again in somewhat different form.* These earlier efforts contributed to creating and sharpening the analytical concepts that finally became the framework for this book. However, what contributed most to this work was the goodwill and frankness of countless Europeans—national government officials in every pertinent EEC capital, officials of the European Communities in Brussels, national and European parliamentarians, party and interest-group leaders, professors, journalists and students. I am also deeply indebted to Jacqueline Lastenouse, who, with charming manner and through vast knowledge of the Brussels Eurocracy, managed all of my EEC interviewing. Numerous colleagues also contributed to my work, and if I identify only a few I hope that the many that remain unnamed will not feel slighted. Glenda Rosenthal was both a constant inspiration and a relentless critic. William Wallace first prompted me to think about fiscal harmonization as an area of inquiry, and Helen Wallace reminded me that the VAT story could not be complete without a British chapter. Carl Lankowski not only collaborated on the German case but also taught me a good deal about European political economy. My research was funded by grants from the Carnegie Endowment for International Peace, the Ford Foundation and the Columbia University Institute on Western Europe. The actual writing of this book was supported by grants from the German Marshall Fund of

* See below, Ch. 3, note 1; Ch. 4, note 1; Ch. 5, note 1. Cf., also, Donald J. Puchala, 'Worm Cans and Worth Taxes: Fiscal Harmonization and the European Policy Process,' in Helen Wallace, William Wallace and Carole Webb (eds), *Policy-making in the European Communities* (London, John Wiley & Sons, 1977), pp. 249–72.

the United States and the Institute of International Studies of the University of South Carolina.

I sincerely thank those who contributed to enhancing this study's strengths. I take sole responsibility for its weaknesses.

DJP
Columbia, South Carolina
January 1984

1
The analysis of international policy-making

This book will undoubtedly be classified, catalogued, shelved and perhaps even read as a study of the Western European Common Market. In a conventional sense it is yet another examination of 'European Integration,' and later chapters will cast some light on the making of decisions in Brussels, the efforts of Eurocrats and the building of consensus among governments. Readers will discover, however, that activities in Brussels and the workings of the institutions of the European Communities are not the main concerns of this particular study of European Integration. Rather, the analytical focus is upon the national governments of EC member countries and their handling of issues and problems thrust upon them as a result of their participation in the Common Market. Moreover, the study is not much concerned with progress toward or slippage away from a political union, or a United States of Europe. For that matter, it is not much concerned with the European Communities for their own sake. Instead, the goal of the research that led to this book was to learn *from* the European Communities rather than to merely learn *about* them. Western Europe's thirty-year post-war experience in international community-building contains countless lessons about the promise and potential, and the problems and pitfalls in international cooperation among Western democracies. The overriding purpose of this book is to extract, display and discuss some of these lessons.

The Western European lessons that are the specific concern of this study have to do with relationships between contests in national politics and capacities for international cooperation. On the one hand the study looks into ways that domestic politics—or competition among individuals, groups and

factions for influence, office or other rewards within countries
—affects governments' abilities to cooperate with one another
internationally. Conversely, it also looks into ways in which
governments' attempts to cooperate internationally affect
politics within countries. We might suppose that national
politics may either further or hinder international cooperation, and that international cooperation may either provoke
or allay national-level politiking. But, the more intriguing
questions have to do with when, how and why? One prime
analytical concern in later substantive chapters will therefore
be to determine the conditions under which, and the extent
to which, constraints imposed, opportunities afforded or
imperatives raised by national domestic politics in EC member
states affect the content, timing and implementation of
internationally-agreed policies and courses of collaborative
action. Another task will be to determine how and why
attempts to formulate or implement common EC policies
affect the fates and fortunes of various political groups and
factions within member states and the political standing of
governments with their domestic supporters and opponents.

Politics, Politicization, Political Will and Political Capacity

Assumptions about politics that guided research and that
underpin analysis in this study are Lasswellian.[1] Political
behavior is gamelike in that it is rational and goal-directed
and evolves in moves and countermoves determined by
strategies. Such behavior is fundamentally conflictual,
although it encompasses the formation of alliances or coalitions for purposes of more effective competition. Political
behavior is directed toward maintaining or enhancing actors'
power to distribute rewards within or between societies.
Attaining political power then is tantamount to being able to
significantly influence 'who gets what, when and how.'

More concretely, and more important to the research at
hand, national politics in Western Europe (or anywhere else)
center on controlling national governments. To attain such
control is to gain considerable sway over the distribution of
material and symbolic rewards in society, and being able to
influence this distribution is the prize in political competition.

The chief political instinct of any ruling group is to act to maintain itself in office, and the primary political drive of any opposition group is to move into office. From this it follows that incumbents and opposition parties must be especially sensitive to issues that might, during debate or upon resolution, affect control over national government by affecting political competitors' respective appeals, resources or power. When otherwise technical issues come to be perceived as affecting the respective fortunes of different groups competing for control over government, such issues are said to be *politicized* and the process by which they come to be thus perceived is called *politicization*. Once politicization has occurred, responses to issues by governments and opposition groups tend to be selected, as much (or more!), for their political appeal as for their technical merit.

Politicization and consequent political competition need not be limited only to interactions between governmental incumbents and outside challengers. They may occur in any situation where the handling of issues could affect the relative status, influence or power of those involved in deliberations. Within political parties, for example, positions on issues might be taken with regard to the technical efficacy of alternative solutions to policy problems. Or, they might be taken with regard to how alternatives would affect the relative status of different intra-party factions or the relative fortunes of different aspirants for leadership. Similarly, within national civil services choices for solutions to problems may follow from considerations about efficiency or cost effectiveness, or, they may have to do with their effects on the relative status or resources of different agencies or individuals in the bureaucratic hierarchy. As a rule, issues are debated and positions are conditioned by both technical and political considerations, but the closer that issues come to affecting participants' status and power, actually or perceptibly, the more highly politicized they become and the less relevant become technical considerations.

'Politicization' is a rather clumsy word. But it is also a powerful concept that offers a key to understanding phenomena examined later in this study. Common policies in the European Communities usually begin as searches for solutions to technical problems by qualified experts concerned with the efficiency, neatness and substantive impact of amalgamating various national practices. However, common EC policies usually reach fruition as complex compromises among national political officials who are frequently less concerned with transnational neatness than with the effects of Community decisions and directives on voters, supporters and political rivals at home. Politicization therefore transforms the nature of EC policy debates, and the way in which it is handled by national governments and Community authorities turns out to be one of the key determinants of the feasibility of common policies, their timing, their substance and their enforceability. This study will show, for example, that the degree of politicization which takes place domestically within EC member states has a great deal to do with whether governments are able to cooperate with one another internationally.

Political Will and Political Capacity

Political will and *political capacity* are similarly useful concepts, although in analyzing the affairs of the European Communities they are often confused. The Commission of the European Communities and the European Parliament tend to attribute most delays and debacles in EC policy-making to failures of 'political will' on the parts of the governments of member countries. If by this they mean that national authorities in Community countries periodically lose their desire to cooperate with one another or with the Commission because perceived national interests dictate independent courses, there have been some instances of failed will in EC experience. British refusal to join the Common Market in the late 1950s was one such instance; President de Gaulle's vetoes prohibiting British admission in the 1960s were other instances; Common Market disunity during the world petroleum crisis in 1974 was another example. Note that these were situations where cooperation did not occur because governments clearly did not want to cooperate.[2] Here conflictual outcomes may properly be attributed to lack of *political will*.

But what is much more common in EC experience is

failure due to *political incapacity*, where governments for domestic political reasons are simply unable to respond to their Community partners in accommodating ways. In such instances there is no lessening of governments' desires to co-operate. Rather, there are real or perceived impediments to their abilities to do so and these are political in nature. That is, governments would cooperate if they could, but they cannot because they perceive the domestic political costs to be prohibitive. For example, in an episode that will be explored in great depth later in this study, when movement toward harmonizing taxes in different EC countries stalled between 1973 and 1975, the European Commission published a report that admonished national governments and called for a show of 'political will' to relaunch the harmonization process.[3] Earlier, in 1972–73 Italy's lagging behind other countries in introducing the Community-wide value-added tax was also popularly attributed to lack of political will, as was Dutch procrastination on tax policy between 1964 and 1967.[4] However, investigation reveals, and later chapters will show, that these and any number of similar episodes were more properly failures of capacity rather than will. Neither the reluctant partners in 1975, nor the Italian Government in 1973 or the Dutch Government in 1964 lacked the will to cooperate toward strengthening the European Common Market. They all wanted this strengthening to occur. But they did lack the political capacity to act toward this goal at different times because they perceived that they could not pursue internationally accommodating positions without jeopardizing their respective holds on domestic political power. On the other hand, because the political will to co-operate has tended to remain pronounced for most EC governments even during the interludes of incapacity, it has proven repeatedly possible for the Communities to resume movement toward greater unity once political incapacities were overcome. Generally speaking, *political will* helps to account for the longer-run continuity of EC policy-making, while *political capacity* has more to do with explaining shorter-run discontinuities. Later chapters will show this.

Political Arenas and Political Reverberation

Like other organized spectacles, political games are played in arenas: these are conventionally called political systems. Such systems are conceptual creations, unreal in any objective sense, but useful if they help the analyst to better understand the identities and juxtapositions of actors whose behavior must be accounted for if political phenomena are to be explained.[5] While there are a number of more or less elegant images of the European Communities as a political system contained in the theoretical literature on international integration, most of these do not adequately focus on linkages between domestic political contests within member-states and relations among governments and between them and Community authorities in Brussels.[6] Therefore, it is worth digressing just a bit at this point to paint a picture of 'Europe.'

To get a perspective on the arena within which events described in later chapters occur it would be helpful to imagine something like an eleven-ring circus, with ten of these rings around the periphery representing the political institutions and activities of the EC member-states, and the eleventh in the center, representing the institutions and activities of the Common Market. For simplicity let us call this center ring 'Brussels.' Now let us imagine a ping-pong table in the center of each ring with contestants poised and ready to play. However, at the start of the game only the contestants in the center ring have a ball. They paddle it back and forth until at some point it gets slapped from the center table and lands on one of the peripheral tables, where the game continues, until, at another point, the ball gets slapped onto another peripheral table, and thus the game continues.

This eleven-ring ping-pong metaphor hardly does justice to the complexity of political interactions in the European Communities, but it underlines several of the key features of the EC political system. If we suppose that the ping-pong ball is an issue that requires a response from the European Communities in the form of a decision concerning common policy, the metaphor suggests that in the EC policy process issues tend to be moved back and forth between Brussels, where they are 'paddled' about by Eurocrats and ministers, and member-countries, where they are contested within and among political parties, factions, interest groups and ministries. In addition, it would seem from the metaphor that the stopping point for the game in one arena is at the same time its starting point in another, so that intermediate outcomes condition the locus and continuation of play. In the same way, the stopping time in one arena is the starting time in another so that intermediate outcomes also condition the tempo of play. Finally, the game is continuous and would appear so to an observer positioned to watch all ten rings simultaneously. However, to players within the separate circles of activity the game appears discontinuous, broken into phases or episodes or otherwise proceeding in fits and starts.

What the metaphor describes in most simple fashion is the process of *political reverberation*, or, the shifting of policy debates back and forth between international and domestic arenas. This is a key to understanding the linkage between national politics and the European Community's policy process. Participating in negotiations toward the international agreements that become the common policies of the European Communities requires that each government formulate positions. This in turn often leads to deliberations and debates in domestic arenas, where politicization usually takes place. As a result, governments are impelled to embrace positions in Brussels that are domestically most advantageous for them. No government wants anything to come out of Brussels that would jeopardize its standing at home, and, ideally, each government would prefer that outcomes in Brussels buttress its standing at home. Once national positions are formulated, negotiations in Brussels juxtapose them and mix them with recommendations from the Commission. This generally yields first-round, or 'intermediate' outcomes, which most frequently take the form of deadlocks among national delegations because some governments conclude that none of the alternatives discussed during the negotiations would be politically palatable at home.

Debate then moves back into domestic arenas where governments may try to reformulate their positions in ways that might make later agreement in Brussels easier. This means trying to modify aspects of their earlier positions that other governments found to be particularly objectionable, and it requires either rallying domestic support for the re-formulated policy or quelling opposition to it. Alternatively, governments may return from Brussels determined to remain firm in their initial positions and intent upon marking time until others change theirs. Later analysis will show that such obduracy is frequently the result of political incapacity since the reluctant government may perceive that any change in its position would expose it to unacceptable domestic political penalties. Meanwhile, the European Commission searches for bases for compromise among governments, prepares new recommendations and prods the EC's inter-governmental organs toward new negotiating sessions. Debate eventually moves back to Brussels, again yields intermediate results (including further deadlock) and then returns once more to domestic arenas where governments try again to sort out their positions. Issues may reverberate politically in this fashion for extended periods of time—seven years on average for major Community decisions—until ultimately compromise and closure become possible. This happens when all member-governments are able to conclude that the negotiations have produced something that they can live with politically at home. When, how and why they reach such conclusions are discussed in later chapters.

But member-governments' conclusions about the domestic palatability of Community policies are sometimes premature. National political uproar may in fact become most intense when the EC sets about attempting to implement policies already negotiated and agreed. It is sometimes only after enforcement is attempted that the politically unsettling impacts of Community decisions are most clearly felt within member-countries. When this happens political reverberation continues into the post-decisional phase of the EC policy process. Negative reactions to Community policies in national arenas frequently force member-governments to delay in implementing them. Such delay constitutes non-compliance, infracts the Treaty of Rome and propels issues back to Brussels for new negotiations between offending governments and the Commission and among governments in the Council of Ministers. As non-compliance is most often the result of political incapacity in one or more domestic arenas, negotiations aimed at bringing offending governments into compliance may yield several intermediate outcomes of the 'no movement at all' variety. The matter will thus continue to reverberate between domestic and international arenas until national political conditions ultimately permit deviant governments to implement the EC policies.

European Integration

Admittedly, it is rather difficult to find very much of Jean Monnet's idealized 'Europe' on the political gaming field depicted here. National governments' responses to Community policies and policy-making appear to range between enthusiasm, indifference and opposition, depending largely upon how these might affect their domestic political fortunes. Governments push towards common policies or block them, implement or ignore or reject them depending upon how much domestic advantage they may bring or how much political discomfort they might cause. In all of this national sovereignty appears scarcely diminished, although it would seem that governments are willing to exchange modicums of their autonomy for the benefits of collectively generated outcomes and for whatever domestic political supports the Communities can offer to them.[7] Supranational authorities appear neither very supranational nor especially authoritative, and Eurocratic efforts to enhance unity among member-states appear to proceed only as far as the least cooperative government is willing to go, and only as fast as the slowest government is willing to move.

But let us not lose perspective. It is true that the dynamics of relations within and between the countries of the European Communities are fundamentally and intensely political. Just how fundamentally and intensely political the workings of the EC really are does not show through very clearly in most analyses of 'European Integration,' and for this reason politics are going to be highlighted in this study. However, the final results of the reverberating political contests that compose the EC policy process often contribute to greater unity and harmony among member-states—i.e., to enhanced integration. Even when harmonization proceeds only as far and as fast as the most cautious governments will permit, it proceeds nevertheless. Community policies may take decades to formulate and implement, but European experience has shown that they are eventually formulated and implemented. The reasons for these integrative results will be examined in later chapters. Some have to do with 'political will' in the form of strong and continuing commitments among EC governments to the worth and promise of collaborative behavior. Others follow from dynamics generated during international negotiations which ultimately make compromise costly to resist. Still others have to do with political sensitivities shared by governments and the astute tactics of the Brussels Eurocracy, which, while it lacks power does not want completely for influence. Ironically, many characteristics of the EC policy process widely interpreted as shortcomings, as for example its tedious tempo, its contingency upon national politics, its exposure to national vetoes, and its 'common denominator' outcomes, turn out upon analysis to be sources of strength. All of them lend durability to the Community and continuity to its inter-governmental processes. Over the long run these are what count most in fostering greater unity. Later chapters will show why this is so.

Studying the Politics of European Integration

Much of the rest of this book is concerned with concretely illustrating the abstract discussion of the politics of European Integration presented here in Chapter 1. After that, the remainder of the work is directed toward probing the workings of the European Communities for lessons and insights that may have broader relevance for understanding international cooperation more generally.

No particular body of social scientific theory informs this study, and it pretends to make no systematic theoretical contribution. Many of its concerns, however, are similar to those of the neofunctional integration theorists, especially its emphasis upon policy processes and politicization.[8] But the neofunctionalists' formulations proved too complex and their analytical vocabulary too obtuse to allow for meaningful analysis of the straightforward information about political tugging and hauling that constitutes the empirical subject matter of this study. Other theoretical influences were eclectically gathered and various concepts and models are employed where useful. As noted earlier, notions about political motivations are Lasswellian. Glimpses of Machiavelli occasionally appear, but more often in domestic than in international contexts. The game theory and game-theoretic vocabulary come of course from the game theorists.[9] The European Communities as depicted in this study still look like a Concordance System.[10] Member-countries of the EC are modeled as pluralist democracies, much as David Truman or Theodore Lowi would perceive them.[11] National bureaucracies are assumed to behave in ways that Graham Allison would readily understand, particularly when he peers through his second conceptual lens.[12] The conceptual vocabulary used in this study—politicization, political will, political capacity and political reverberation—was created more for convenience than for profundity. Each term captures a very complex phenomenon in shorthand form, and as such each summarizes and symbolizes a quality or process that will be the constant focus of analytical attention throughout the study.

The book also employs a narrative vocabulary that warrants an introductory note so that later confusion might be avoided. Officially, the ten-member European organization that is the focus of this study is called The European Communities; it is the present-day amalgam of what were once the European Coal and Steel Community, the European Economic Community and the European Atomic Energy Community. The European Economic Community is also sometimes called the European Common Market or simply the Common Market, and abbreviated as the EEC, while the European Communities are sometimes referred to as the European Community or the Community and abbreviated as the EC. At the cost of some technical inaccuracy, but to avoid tedious repetition and grammatical gymnastics in later chapters, all of the names for The European Communities are used interchangeably. In addition, Brussels is the capital of Belgium and the seat of the Belgian Government, but it is also the headquarters of The European Communities and the home of its primary policy-making institutions, the European Commission and the European Council of Ministers. Therefore, as used in this book 'Brussels' means the Community institutions, or the political arena within which national governments interact with the Community institutions. Context will always indicate exactly which meaning of Brussels is intended. Finally, 'Europe,' as used here refers to the union of states and peoples envisaged and valued by those who initiated and those who continue to believe in European Integration. These people are called 'Europeans.' In this book we remove the quotation marks, again largely to avoid tediousness, but unless context clearly indicates otherwise, 'Europe' and 'European' are employed in their philosophical senses.

This book has four objectives. First, the study reported in the next several chapters attempts to lend empirical meaning to its central analytical concepts and to learn as much about the phenomena they describe as observation and inference will permit. That is, how do we identify politicization, political will, political capacity and political reverberation in the workings of the European Communities, and what are the nature, causes and consequences of these phenomena?

Second, the study attempts to push an enhanced understanding of politicization, political will, political capacity and political reverberation toward improving our understanding of relationships between domestic politics in the member-states of the European Communities and international diplomacy in Brussels. How do constraints, opportunities and imperatives in the domestic politics of member-states affect the content, timing and impacts of the European Community's policies and programs? Conversely, how do the formulation and implementation of Community-wide policies and programs affect the substance, intensity and results of domestic political contests in EC member-states?

Third, the study undertakes to illustrate and explain how linkages between domestic politics in EC member-states and international diplomacy in Brussels affect the process of of 'European Integration,' which here shall mean collaboration among governments that results in collective programs addressed to solving transnational problems.

Fourth, and perhaps most importantly, the study attempts to derive lessons from the experience of European Integration about more general relationships between domestic politics and international cooperation. In particular, we shall want to learn as much as observation and inference will permit about domestic conditions that either support or hamper international cooperation. We shall seek further insights into ways that governments perceive and react to domestic political developments in partner countries and how such perceptions and reactions affect international collaboration. In addition, we will want to examine the influences of international institutions, and particularly international bureaucracies that intermittently insert themselves into both domestic politics at the national level and diplomacy at the international. Do such agents help or hinder international cooperation?

Four Variations on a Theme

The substantive chapters that follow concern the Common Market's twenty-one-year-long attempt to harmonize turnover taxes across member-countries. As explained in Chapter 2, the drive toward fiscal harmonization, a key component in economic integration, began with tasks assigned to the European Commission in the Treaty of Rome in 1958. It has not yet yielded final, or even overly impressive results. By 1979, when this book's case studies end, the Communities had instituted a common form of turnover, or sales, tax—the Value Added Tax or VAT—and member-governments had agreed about the common 'bundle of goods and services' that would be subject to the tax. However, not all countries had as yet actually begun taxing the 'common bundle,' and the ultimate goal of taxing similar items at similar rates throughout the Common Market was still distant (and remains so today). Beyond the turnover tax, common excise taxes on commodities such as tobacco, alcohol and petroleum remained under discussion, where they had been for years, and common corporate and individual income taxes were relegated to the indefinite future.

Though it is rather interesting in its technical complexities, fiscal harmonization was selected as the substantive focus of this study mainly because it is an example of the making and implementation of a Community-wide common policy. For reasons discussed in a moment the fiscal harmonization experience is a rather good example of the European Communities in operation for the particular purposes of this study. But other illustrative cases could easily have been selected, like the formulation and implementation of the Common Agricultural Policy, or one or more of the many sub-policies within the CAP, or the Fisheries Policy or Competition policy, or any number of other areas where national practices and legislation have had to be adjusted and fit into a community-wide regime. Admittedly, nothing in this study establishes the representativeness of fiscal harmonization in the EC's policy-making experience, and nothing therefore guarantees the generalizability of findings. It is for this reason that theoretical contributions were earlier disclaimed. Until further studies are conducted, using concepts and following data-gathering and analytical procedures that replicate those employed here, results from this study must remain tentative. But it is hoped that the reader finds them interesting none the less.

Looking at taxes and at attempts to reform, impose and ultimately internationalize them well suited the purposes of this study because tax issues bring out very basic political responses. People get agitated about taxes and their differing interests in creating or abolishing, continuing or changing, or raising or lowering them are usually clearly defined and easily observed. These interests are most often noisily and colorfully expressed in political arenas! Because tax questions are readily politicized and thus provoke lively politics, they make highly appropriate subjects for a study designed to probe into relationships between national politics and international cooperation.

The fiscal harmonization process in the EC is also a useful and revealing subject for this study because it yielded a variety of outcomes, all of which may be taken as dependent variables demanding explanation. In the most general way, the fiscal harmonization drive in the European Communities between 1958 and 1979 may be described as a success that resulted from a long series of failures. The drive was successful inasmuch as there was a great deal more commonality in national tax systems in 1979 than there was in 1958, and this was largely because of EC efforts. Why and how this came about can, should and will be explained in terms of the concepts that frame this study. Yet, the movement to get even a single common tax, the VAT, took over two decades, and it is not yet complete. During this time most major deadlines in the Commission's timetable were missed, the entire movement stalled absolutely on several occasions, and the final product differs significantly from the one that the Commission initially preferred. Why and how all of this came about also can, should and will be explained in terms of the concepts that frame this study.

Technically, the study is a four-way comparative case analysis of experiences with Community-mandated fiscal harmonization in the Federal Republic of Germany, the Netherlands, Italy and the United Kingdom. The movement to create and apply a turnover tax for the entire European Community affected all four of these member-states similarly, and, for that matter, all of the rest as well save France. In each country the question of adopting a new tax was rapidly and intensely politicized, thus creating problems for respective national governments that had to be resolved domestically before any international action could be taken toward meeting the Community's goal of abolishing fiscal frontiers. Politicization at the national level then is the common theme that runs through each country's experience. But, how and when political pressures developed, how they were handled, why, and with what results, and how domestic political contests affected Community interactions all differed from country to country and from case to case. There were therefore any number of very interesting variations on the theme of politicization and its results. The four countries included in the study were selected precisely because their experiences nicely illustrate these variations.

Research procedures employed were confessedly

old-fashioned. Documents were studied and people were interviewed. Since most of the political tugging and hauling that is part and parcel of any public policy-making process tend to get sterilized out of official documents, interviews were crucially important. These were conducted over a number of years, in Bonn in 1972, in Rome in 1974, in The Hague in 1976, in London in 1982, and in Brussels repeatedly during the entire period and most recently in 1983. For each national episode investigated, an attempt was made to identify and interview each of the key national civil servants, political figures or interest group representatives involved in relevant negotiations or political contests. Similarly, the respondents sought out in Brussels were those officials from the Commission, the Council Secretariat and respective national delegations that personally participated in the events under investigation. Except for officials at the level of Minister or Commissioner, who were inaccessible, and a few others who had gone into retirement abroad of who had passed away, most respondents sought after were reached and interviewed. Interviews were open-ended and conversational. No standard instrument was used since each respondent was specifically questioned about his or her participation in the events under investigation and about the motivations, perceptions and reflections that accompanied such participation. In all, nearly 200 people contributed insights and eye-witness accounts. Without their candidness and goodwill this study could not have been conducted.

The book extends to seven chapters. Chapter 2 delves a bit into the notion of fiscal harmonization, its general contribution to economic integration and its specific part in European economic integration. The chapter then looks into some of the technicalities of turnover taxation and the mechanism of the Value Added Tax. It does this not to make readers into tax experts but to lay the foundations for later political analyses. Unless one understands the nature of the issues that are being politically contested, it is difficult to understand either why the contest is happening or who is prevailing. Chapter 2 concludes with a review of the twenty-one-year fiscal harmonization drive in the EC looked at from the perspective of the outside observer. Analysis in other chapters will reveal that the drive looked different to each of the actors involved.

Chapters 3, 4, 5 and 6 are detailed case studies of German, Dutch, Italian and British experiences with the Value Added Tax. They concretely illustrate the central theme of politicization and its variations and give empirical meaning to political will, political capacity and political reverberation. These chapters are the substantive heart of the study. Each is in its own right a rather interesting morsel of national political history.

Chapter 7, finally, sums up and generalizes. Here lessons about international cooperation learned from the experiences of the European Communities are identified, displayed, discussed and pondered. How interesting it would be if we could conclude some 150 pages from now that it was really worth studying the political behavior of irate shopkeepers, status-conscious treasury officials, party whips and price-wary housewives because it taught us something important about international cooperation.

Notes

1. Harold D. Lasswell, *Politics: Who Gets What, When, How*, Cleveland, The World Publishing Company, 1958.
2. Miriam Camps, *Britain and the European Community*, Princeton, Princeton University Press, 1964, *passim*; Nora Beloff, *The General Says No*, Baltimore, Penguin Books, 1963, *passim.*; Robert J. Lieber, *Oil and the Middle East War: Europe and the Energy Crisis*, Cambridge, Mass., Harvard Center for International Affairs, 1976, *passim*.
3. Agence Internationale D'Information Pour La Presse, *Europe Documents* [hereafter cited as *Europe Documents*], No. 861, 9/10/75; Agence Internationale D'Information Pour La Presse, *Europe* [hereafter cited as *Agence Europe*], 11/22/75, p. 1.
4. Donald J. Puchala, 'European Fiscal Harmonization: Politics During the Dutch Interlude,' in *Contemporary Perspectives on European Integration*, Leon Hurwitz (ed.), Westport, Conn., Greenwood Press, 1980, pp. 209–24.
5. David Easton, *The Political System*, New York, Alfred A. Knopf, 1953, *passim*.
6. One of the most sophisticated attempts to model the political

system of the European Communities is to be found in Leon N. Lindberg and Stuart A. Scheingold, *Europe's Would-Be Polity*, Englewood Cliffs, N.J., Prentice-Hall, 1970, pp. 64–100.

7. For a discussion of 'autonomy' and 'sovereignty' in the EC context, see Donald Puchala and Hugh Balaam, 'National Autonomy and the European Communities,' a paper presented at the International Conference on European Integration, John F. Kennedy Center, Tilburg, 1978.

8. Ernst B. Haas, 'International Integration: The European and the Universal Process,' *International Organization*, Vol. 15, No. 3 (Summer 1961), pp. 366–92; Ernst B. Haas and Philippe C. Schmitter, 'Economics and Differential Patterns of Political Integration: Projections about Unity in Latin America,' *International Organization*, Vol. 18, No. 4 (Autumn 1964), pp. 705–37.

9. See, for example, Thomas C. Schelling, *The Strategy of Conflict*, Cambridge, Mass., Harvard University Press, 1960.

10. Donald J. Puchala, 'Of Blind Men, Elephants and International Integration,' *Journal of Common Market Studies*, Vol. 10, No. 3 (March 1972), pp. 267–84.

11. David Truman, *The Governmental Process*, New York, Alfred Knopf, 1951; Theodore Lowi, 'Making Democracy Safe for the World: National Politics and Foreign Policy,' in *Domestic Sources of Foreign Policy*, James N. Rosenau (ed.), New York, The Free Press, 1967, pp. 295–332.

12. Graham T. Allison, *Essence of Decision*, Boston, Little, Brown and Company, 1971.

2

Fiscal harmonization in theory and practice

The European Common Market is presently more than a customs union, but less than an economic union. During the quarter-century of the European Economic Community's existence its six, then nine and now ten members, prodded by the European Commission, have been integrating their economies. Slowly, but indeed surely, they have been creating among themselves what they formally call an Economic and Monetary Union. When completed it will entail:

(A) the unrestricted movement of goods and services across intra-Community national frontiers, together with the harmonization of government policies designed to prevent the distortion of markets;

(B) the unrestricted movement of factors of production such as labor, capital and technology, and the co-ordination of national policies to ensure that the allocation of resources is based upon highest marginal productivity within the Community; and

(C) fixed or closely aligned exchange rates among Community currencies together with unlimited convertibility, a common monetary policy, the common determination of economic policy and a system of intra-Community transfers.[1] Europeans of the neofunctionalist persuasion see Economic and Monetary Union as one dimension of a more comprehensive political federation.[2]

Harmonization

The Europeans' ultimate goals, however, have been relegated to the distant future. The common market that member governments committed themselves to when they signed the

Treaty of Rome in 1957 is not yet finished, and anything beyond is in the realm of aspirations only. The customs union is nearly complete: most tariffs and quantitative restrictions on intra-Community trade have been removed, and a common external tariff is in place. Nevertheless, a great deal remains to be accomplished toward freeing movements of goods and services, and harmonizing government policies to prevent market distortions. As it turns out, tariffs and quotas are only the most obvious impediments to trade and distorters of markets. Once these are removed other 'non-tariff' barriers become more visible and market-distorting, as for example 'domestic content' laws of various kinds, preferential treatment accorded to national companies on public works projects, nationally peculiar labelling and packaging requirements and restrictive national health and veterinary codes. At the same time, governments, prodded by special interests or sensitized by difficult economic condi-tion, can usually find ways to subsidize national exporters so that they can undersell competitors on foreign markets regardless of patterns of natural comparative advantage. It has not been unusual, for example, for governments to be highly generous in 'rebating' domestic taxes paid on exported commodities.

Though less heralded than the periodic grand initiatives toward greater economic unity, like the Common Agricul-tural Policy, the European Monetary Union or the European Monetary System, the most persistent market-integrating efforts of the European Community have been programs aimed at removing market distortions caused by non-tariff barriers. In particular, the authorities in Brussels have been anxious to combat national proclivities to bestow trading advantages on national firms and sectors by favoring them in legislation or regulatory practice. By promoting what is technically termed 'harmonization' the European Commis-sion has sought to eliminate artificial trading advantages and disadvantages by assimilating the legislative parameters of economic activities in the different member-states. That is, to the extent possible, the Commission strives to insure that competitors within any EC member-state compete under similar regulatory conditions and within similar legal frameworks whatever their country of origin and wherever their business takes place. In practice this has meant directing changes in national laws or administrative practices that discriminate against non-nationals or otherwise offer advantages to national firms. Sometimes such harmonization has involved replacing divergent national practices completely by substituting Community-wide regimes (i.e., common EC policies) that member-governments are directed to write into national law.

Harmonization is a highly technical and rather tedious procedure, particularly when it takes the form of devising and instituting broad Community policies to standardize national practices in economic sectors. It is initiated by research into market-distorting practices, which is followed by wide-ranging consultations with national governments, interest group representatives and technical experts. These are directed toward finding acceptable formulas for aligning divergent national laws and regulations. Eventually, the Commission presents proposed harmonizing formulas to the Council of Ministers in the form of draft directives. When approved by the Council, the directives enter into force and the member-governments to whom they are addressed are obliged to comply. Most do. Compliance, however, is monitored by the Commission which is empowered under the Treaty of Rome to pursue infractors and to bring their cases before the European Court of Justice if necessary.

Harmonization is often also an intensely political process. Since the substance of national laws and regulatory practices frequently reflects past legislative or intra-bureaucratic compromises, or balances of factional power that prevailed at the time of passage, calls for change can reopen old political contests. Such calls for change are precisely what directives from the European Communities amount to. Either particular countries are asked to change their laws, or the entire group of member-states is so directed. In each instance a national political status quo is shaken and domestic contests begin over how, when and whether national adjustments should be made to comply with EC directives. Or, in a more complicated but also more realistic way, the domestic political contests actually begin in anticipation of Community directives, when interest groups and factions approach national governments to try to influence the content of the draft directives. Naturally, the most acceptable kinds of directives from the Community are those that ask people to do what they would want to do anyway, and these are the kinds that national interest groups hope that their governments will bring home from Brussels. The politiking generally continues through the decisional process that produces directives—i.e., while the Commission is preparing its drafts, while it consults the Council and while the Council deliberates. Then, similar contests are engaged to influence the interpretation of directives and these continue well on into the period during which directives are being nationally implemented. Tension is inherent in this process because for most governments the path of least political resistance is the one that calls for the least change in national practices. Yet, the divergences in national practices are often so great that harmonization requires considerable change and therefore the path of least political resistance must necessarily be closed to some governments. *Who is going to be asked to change how much*, then, is always at issue when the Community moves toward common policies.

Fiscal Harmonization

The relationship between fiscal harmonization and economic union is uncomplicated. A common market is less than common to the extent that different participants maintain differing fiscal regimes. Taxes affect manufacturers' costs of production, financiers' investment strategies and consumers' preferences, and to the extent that fiscal regimes diverge among states of a customs union the differing economic conditions they create can affect patterns of trade. More importantly, in light of issues already raised in this chapter, national taxes imposed on imports, or rebated on exports, or both, can raise barriers to trade or otherwise distort international competition, sometimes to the extent of cancelling liberalizations achieved through the elimination of tariffs and quotas. The trade-distorting effects of fiscal frontiers are reinforced when governments deliberately engage in manipulating taxes for protectionist reasons. As noted, such practices are not exactly unknown.

The drafters of the Rome Treaty saw clearly that movement toward fiscal harmonization had to go hand-in-hand with the removal of tariffs and the elimination of quotas as Europe's customs union evolved toward more complete economic union. Five articles in the Treaty set the stage for the fiscal harmonization drive:

1. Article 95 prohibits Community member-states from imposing taxes on imports at rates in excess of those imposed upon similar products produced domestically;
2. Article 96 prohibits member-states from subsidizing exports through inflated tax rebates;
3. Article 97 sets standards for tax rebates on exports and empowers the Commission to enforce these standards;
4. Article 98 stipulates varieties of taxes which may and may not be used to affect imports and exports;
5. Article 99 calls for a harmonization of the fiscal regimes of member-states in the realm of indirect or turnover taxation—i.e., those taxes that most directly affected intra-EEC trade because they were rebated and imposed as goods crossed national frontiers. The Article asks the Commission to 'consider how the legislation of the various Member States concerning turnover taxes . . . can be harmonized in the interest of the common market.' It foresaw a Community-wide turnover tax with similar rates for similar goods and services in all member-states, and in this the ultimate elimination of intra-Community fiscal frontiers. Articles 95–98, then, established transitional procedures intended to control abuses of fiscal frontiers until such a time as the harmonization prescribed in Article 99 could be accomplished.[3]

Fiscal harmonization among EC member-states was initially deemed important as a step toward eliminating market distortions. But, it later assumed significance in two additional senses. By 1970 member-governments were prepared to endorse Commission proposals that the European Communities should become self-financing. This transition to financial autonomy had been foreseen in Article 207 of the

Rome Treaty. Accordingly, in its Decision of 21 April 1970, the Council of Ministers set down that from 1975 onward the direct assessment of member-states would cease and the Community budget would be financed from the EC's 'own resources.' These were to include receipts from customs duties, revenues generated by agricultural levies and *up to one percent of a community-wide turnover tax collected on a common base of goods and services in each of the member-states.*[4] Fiscal harmonization thus became linked to Community budgeting and the 'own resources' scheme, and, in the web of EC institutional initiatives, it was intended that financing from 'own resources' would precede or at least coincide with the seating of the first directly elected European Parliament. In this way fiscal harmonization became one of the prerequisites to some rather ambitious projected integrative undertakings.

Fiscal harmonization also became an element in the Community's drive toward Economic and Monetary Union (EMU), the first major push beyond the specific mandates of the Rome Treaty. At The Hague Summit in December 1969, the Community's political leaders committed themselves to movement toward a complete economic union which would include monetary integration and the centralization of economic policy-making. Neither of these moves had been specifically foreseen in the Rome Treaty. After the Summit, Pierre Werner, Prime Minister of Luxembourg, chaired an inter-governmental committee that worked to prepare precise plans for creating an EMU. The *Werner Report* was intensely debated by Community bodies and much of it was formalized and adopted by the Council of Ministers in the historic Resolution of 21 March 1971 which launched the EMU project.[5] More rapid fiscal harmonization was specifically called for in the Resolution 'in order that effectively free movement of persons, goods, services and capital may be achieved at a faster rate.' In particular, during the first three years of the EMU project the basis for assessing the Community's common turnover tax was to be standardized and plans were to be laid for the alignment of rates. Steps were also to be taken during the early phases of the EMU to harmonize other indirect and direct taxes. In this way, fiscal harmonization became integral to Europe's transition from a customs union to something greater.

But there was an even deeper significance to fiscal harmonization in the context of the EMU. Since the Werner Committee was ultimately unable to reconcile differences between those governments like France and Belgium that wanted to proceed toward Economic and Monetary Union by beginning with the fixing of exchange rates and the elaboration of a common monetary system, and those like West Germany and the Netherlands that wanted to begin with the centralization of economic policy-making, the final report called for parallel steps in both 'monetarist' and 'economic' directions. Thus, to avoid destructive controversy between monetarists and economists as the EMU plan took shape, monetary coordination had to be paralleled by accomplishments in harmonization, which symbolized economic coordination. As guarantor of this parallelism, the Commission hoped that fiscal harmonization could be one of the strong wagons on the *economic* track which would roll steadily along while the monetarists designed their exchange-rate 'snakes' and sent them wriggling through various 'tunnels.' Conceptually then, fiscal harmonization came to mean a great deal to the European Communities between 1971 and 1974. But here we get ahead of our story. The important point is that after 1971 fiscal harmonization took on enhanced respectability and a bit more urgency because it was specifically included in the EMU scheme.

The Value Added Tax

By the time the EMU was launched the European Communities already had a common turnover tax, the Value Added Tax, or VAT. What exactly a Value Added Tax is, and when, how and why this particular tax became the community-wide tax envisaged in the Rome Treaty are all essential elements of background and context to the case studies of national experience with the VAT presented in later chapters. Equally important is the record of what happened to the VAT as a result of the enlargement of the Communities in 1973 and what became of the early planners' image of abolished fiscal frontiers.

Some Prerequisites for Fiscal Harmonization

The rub from the very beginning of the Community's efforts at fiscal harmonization was that according to Article 99 of the Rome Treaty the adoption of a common tax regime required *unanimous* action by the Council of Ministers. Hence, any government displeased with any aspect of the project could cast a veto and thereby stall the enterprise. Consequently, any scheme or formula that the Commission proposed had to fit with the perceived national interests of six governments (later nine). This meant that national sovereignties had to be respected: a Community tax could be nothing more than an assimilated set of national taxes, nationally legislated and nationally collected. Any threat to national taxing authority would have drawn immediate vetoes. Secondly, any threat to national revenues was also unacceptable and had to be avoided in the Community formula. A new tax therefore had to raise as much revenue as any existing one that it replaced in the different member-states, and there could be no doubts about this beforehand. Third, any new fiscal regime suggested by the Commission had to provide national governments with the political and financial wherewithal to overcome those vested interests that benefited under existing national fiscal regimes and that would certainly protest strongly if these were changed. In almost every EC member-country political pressures, contests, compromises and post-electoral rewards over the years had created systems of tax favors and exemptions that could not be snatched from their beneficiaries without political costs. Therefore, an acceptable Community tax had either to minimize these domestic political costs to national governments, or, better still, to provide governments with resources that could be distributed at home as political rewards. Fourth, even without the conservative inertia of existing fiscal regimes, the Commission still faced the task of finding a new turnover tax which offended no national fiscal tradition either in principle or in substance, and the fiscal traditions of each of the Six were quite different as regards indirect taxation.[6] Finally, the Community tax had to be one that national ministries of finance were administratively capable of collecting, and, at the outset every country, save France, had at least some misgivings on administrative grounds.[7]

Naturally, the tax also had to suit the purpose of Community-wide harmonization. As such, it had to be the instrument that would eventually abolish fiscal frontiers among member-states at least as far as turnover levies were concerned. This meant first that it had to be commonly applicable, or, in other words that taxable 'baskets' of goods and services could be defined, that the contents of these baskets were available in every member-state, and that all national governments would be willing to allow the same basket items to be taxed. Eventually, these items would all have to be taxed at similar rates throughout the Community to thus eliminate the need for rebates and reimpositions at national borders. But, since movement toward the standard-ization of national baskets and rates necessarily had to be gradual, the initial technical requirement for the tax was that it had to be *transparent*. There could be no question about how much any given good or service had been taxed, or how much of the selling price represented taxes paid and passed on to consumers. Until the time when common baskets were similarly taxed, goods and services crossing national borders would be 'untaxed' and 'retaxed.' Turnover taxes that had been paid in the country of origin would be rebated to ex-porters, where, simultaneously, taxes prevailing in the country of destination would be imposed and levied on importers. Therefore, if there were anything uncertain or *opaque* about the tax content of the prices of different items the way would be left open for governments to continue to use turnover taxes as export subsidies or non-tariff barriers. This is precisely what fiscal harmonization was supposed to remedy: transparency was the prescription.

The Experts and the Value Added Tax

Faced with these technical and political conditions, the Euro-pean Commission chose to move slowly and cautiously towards finding a turnover tax that would meet all of the criteria of acceptability. The first step would be to compare national practices in turnover taxation and to search out areas of convergence or common denominators that could be the bases for harmonization. Then, when a new scheme was tentatively arrived at, the Commission would attempt to build support among fiscal and financial experts throughout the Community and thus to mobilize pressures on national governments from within national bureaucracies and among national academic and interest group elites. Only after such support had been mobilized behind a Community plan would the Commission put the scheme to the Council of Ministers, which, it was supposed, would bend with the supportive political breeze and readily incorporate it into Community legislation.

Between 1959 and 1962 the Commission's strategy appeared to be succeeding. In 1959 EEC authorities set up a working group of national fiscal experts to assess the impacts on Community trade of the differing systems of indirect taxation in operation in the member-states. Not surprisingly, the report of 'Working Group Number One,' released in December 1959, revealed substantial distortions in trade apparently caused by national manipulations of tax rebates to exporters and various import substitution taxes.[8] The West German Government, to take an example, annually adjusted its import substitution tax, the *Umsatzaugleichsteuer* to protect against iron and steel imports from France.[9] Working Group Number One therefore concluded that something had to be done to reduce such distortions of trade, and the Commission promptly charged three more overlapping study groups—Working Groups A, B and C—with the task of evaluating alternative strategies for Community-wide fiscal harmonization. Almost at the same moment, in April 1960, the Commission created another special committee to look into ways and means of fiscal harmonization. This was a group of sixteen academic experts under the chairmanship of Professor Fritz Neumark of Frankfurt. Meanwhile, in July 1960 member-governments were prompted by the Commission to adopt the so-called *Standstill Agreement*, whereby they agreed not to raise either import substitution taxes or export rebates until the fiscal reviews were completed.[10] This agreement proved tenuous at best as national governments were reluctant to resist protectionist pressures from powerful interest groups.[11]

The working groups and the Neumark Committee all reported in July 1962.[12] Both sets of studies endorsed a Community Value Added Tax as the appropriate route to fiscal harmonization. This form of turnover tax assesses only the value added to raw materials as they become finished products, or the value added to such products as they move from manufacturers through wholesalers to retailers to consumers. A Value Added Tax may also be assessed on services, and it is normally paid by the consumers of such. In a VAT system, during intermediate transactions, 'value added' is calculated as the difference between the price paid for inputs or components (minus whatever tax had been previously paid) and the price charged for the processed goods as they are passed to the next marketing stage. To prevent the 'cascading' of taxes, where prices at each stage include taxes previously paid, VAT payments are rebated to intermediate consumers, and only final consumers are obliged to pay the full tax. Accounting in the VAT system is based upon invoices that separately record prices and tax assessments. These become both the instruments for calculating value added and the sources of documentation for claimed rebates. VAT regimes are conceptually and technically complex, difficult to administer, time-consuming for book-keepers, and rather frightening to taxpayers first exposed to them.

But a VAT has the twin virtues of being almost totally transparent and very difficult to evade. Its transparency makes it particularly appropriate for transactions in international trade. As the *Neumark Report* explained, with payments distributed among stages of production and exchange in such a way that no one pays taxes on taxes already paid, import substitution levies and export rebates can be calculated with great accuracy. These would effect only the value added by the exporter. Moreover, any eventual standardization of the rates of the VAT, product by product and country by country would automatically amount to the abolition of fiscal frontiers since substitution taxes and export rebates would no longer be necessary. With regard to evasion, rebating VAT payments to intermediate processors makes it unrewarding, and the record-keeping required under the invoice system would make it difficult in any event. National treasury officials could appreciate these VAT virtues.

The First and Second VAT Directives

Moving toward a Community-wide Value Added Tax in the early 1960s represented an ambitious EC policy thrust because the VAT form was not a 'common denominator' among national turnover taxes. Only France among the Community member states had a Value Added Tax at that time. The other five had a variety of cascade taxes that were unsuitable to be turned into Community-wide taxes because of their opaqueness. For five of the Six therefore, harmonization would mean introducing a completely new and nationally-untried turnover tax system. Naturally, this was going to have both technical and political implications in the five countries. It might be suspected that choosing the French tax to be the Community tax might have been a gesture of the European Commission taken to avoid difficulties with Paris during a sensitive period of Gaullist rethinking about French participation in the EEC. Research, however, turned up no evidence of this. Rather, the Commission selected the VAT largely on its technical merits.

By October 1962 the Commission was ready with a proposal to the Council of Ministers advocating a phased introduction of a Community VAT to be implemented in all member-states by 1970.[13] But at this point the Council said 'no,' and there ensued a deadlock in Community decision-making that lasted until the summer of 1965.[14] Even though there had been some negative vibrations concerning a Community VAT at the meeting of finance ministers at Echternach in July 1962, the Commission imagined that its proposals would gain easy acceptance because they included elements designed to please everybody. Instead, as it turned out, almost everyone was offended by one element or another. The Dutch rejected the very principle of a multi-stage VAT. The French were quite content with the Value Added Tax already operating in their country and saw no need for revisions directed by EC authorities. The Italians looked upon the VAT as an administrative nightmare. The Belgians would go along only if the Dutch and Germans did. For their part the Germans saw unnecessary delays in the Commission's phased scheme and demanded a faster-moving program.

Even more critical in the autumn and winter of 1962 than the absence of ministerial consensus, was the absence of national political leadership to push fiscal harmonization forward. To this point the enterprise was almost wholly a Commission venture. No national government was as yet either willing or able to champion the goal of a Community VAT, or, for that matter, a Community turnover tax of any kind. Experience even in these years of the Common Market's infancy was beginning to show that it was not enough for the Commission alone to want something integrative to happen in the EC. At least one national government also had to want it, and that government had to take the lead in making it happen. Specifically, in 1962 and for sometime afterward, both the French and the West Germans held back, even though leadership in the fiscal harmonization field had to come from either Paris or Bonn. As the major traders in the Community, their attitudes towards the VAT, one way or the other, would leave their smaller partners with little choice. But in the early 1960s the French Gaullists could hardly be expected to promote proposals for greater European Integration. Nor were the West Germans yet ready to push for a VAT at the Community level, since, as Chapter 3 shows, they themselves had not settled on its acceptability in Germany.

By the spring of 1964, however, the West German Government had become both willing and able to lead the push toward a Community VAT. As it turned out, by this time political developments within Germany had created a context in which the Bonn Government felt the need for a Community VAT even more urgently than the Commission. The result was a new coalition to support the Value Added Tax composed of West German Finance Minister Dahlgrün, EEC Commissioner Hans von der Groeben, and officials from the Commission's Directorate-General for Competition and Bonn's Ministry of Finance. West German advocacy (plus some lightly-veiled threats about agricultural pricing) sufficed to dull Dutch opposition.[15] This, plus promised special considerations with regard to retail trade, helped to ease Italian reluctance. Belgium was still willing to go along if Germany and the Netherlands moved, and since France already had a VAT Paris was not prepared to raise major obstacles. The beginnings of intergovernmental consensus on the VAT showed at the February 1964 meeting of EC finance ministers in Rome, where both the Belgians and the Italians expressed positive attitudes and the Dutch voiced no strong objections. Then, in June 1964, the Commission put revised proposals before the Council that called upon national parliaments to adopt the VAT by 1968 and to arrange for its implementation no later than 1 January 1970. At this time the Commission also pledged to have a second set of proposals ready by the spring of 1965 which would explain in detail exactly how national laws had to be amended to accommodate the new Community tax.

Despite strong German prodding, action by the Council of Ministers was not immediately forthcoming. It was not until April 1965 that the Council finally accepted the principle of a Value Added Tax for the EEC. At this time the Council had two draft directives to consider, the *First VAT Directive*, which established the principle of a Community VAT and set forth the timetable for its implementation, and the *Second VAT Directive* which set down the form and content for legislation that would institute the VAT in the member-states. Neither Directive was adopted in 1965, and the year ended with member-governments able to agree only that if there were going to be a Community-wide turnover tax it should be of the value-added variety.

Although numerous meetings concerning the two draft VAT Directives took place within the Committee of Permanent Representatives (COREPER) and at all technical levels during 1966, apparent inaction on fiscal harmonization continued though the year and on into 1967. In Chapter 4 this period of deadlock, 1964 to 1967, will be called the 'Dutch interlude,' because it was the negative position of the Dutch Government that paralyzed the Council of Ministers. But when Dutch objections were withdrawn in February

1967 the way was finally cleared for the introduction of the VAT. The First and Second VAT Directives were adopted by the Council in April 1967, and 1 January 1970 was set as the date by which all member-states were to begin collecting the new EEC tax.[16]

Four of the Six member-states met the deadline for implementing the new Value Added Tax: France in 1967, Germany in 1968, the Netherlands in 1969 and Luxembourg in 1970. Belgium had to delay one year before falling into step with its partners.[17] Italy, however, could not comply in 1970, 1971 or 1972, and it was not until January 1973 that the Italian Government finally implemented the VAT Directives. As early as the spring of 1969 the Italian Government had made known its intention to postpone the VAT for two years.[18] In September 1969 the Commission reluctantly accepted Italy's request for postponement, but Commissioner von der Groeben criticized 'certain Community member-states for trying to turn the European Communities into an organization like the OECD where members could do as they pleased.'[19] Bargaining between the Commission and the Italian Government (with some rather unsubtle interventions by other Community member-states) yielded a compromise in December 1969 on the conditions for postponement.[20] The new date for the introduction of the Italian VAT was set for January 1972. But, by the spring of 1971 it was clear that Italy was going to request yet another postponement, this time until July 1972. Then, as the July 1972 deadline approached, the Italian Government once more asked for additional time, as the summer tourist season seemed to Rome to be an inopportune period in which to impose a new price-inflating sales tax. The Commission again demurred; 1 January 1973 became the new due date, and the Rome Government was able to meet this deadline. Exactly why the Italian Government was forced to delay the VAT for so long is discussed in detail in Chapter 5.

The Sixth VAT Directive

The first day of January 1973 also marked the first enlargement of the European Communities: the United Kingdom, Ireland and Denmark became members. The treaties of accession obligated the new members to introduce the Community VAT in their countries by 1975, in time for the planned transition to the 'own resources' system for financing the Community budget. Also, at the beginning of 1973, the movement toward Economic and Monetary Union was still very much alive, and with the Value Added Tax finally in force in all of the original Six countries, the Commission hoped that rapid steps could be taken towards standardizing bases and aligning rates as called for in the EMU plan. The new members would be called upon to assimilate such further steps. The United Kingdom introduced a Value Added Tax in April 1973; Ireland and Denmark also had VAT systems operating in that year.

But the Community faltered in its hoped-for rapid steps toward standardizing the Value Added Taxes of the different member-states. The Commission's proposals for what eventually became the Sixth VAT Directive were before the Council of Ministers in the spring of 1973. These contained the list of goods and services that were to be the common basis for assessing the Community VAT in the member-states. But a tour of national finance ministries by EC tax Commissioner Henri Simonet revealed that the national governments were far apart on questions of further fiscal harmonization so that deliberations over the Sixth Directive were likely to be lengthy. They lasted for five years! Among the major sticking points were British insistences that food and certain other everyday 'necessities' should not be included in the common base of the VAT. Such items were not taxed in the United Kingdom, London explained, and could not be taxed there because of political commitments that British governments had made to voters. These commitments, discussed in detail in Chapter 6, forced the British Government into an inflexible stance against the Sixth VAT Directive, much to the chagrin of the Commission and to the displeasure of some of the other governments.

Meanwhile, all of the deadlines in the fiscal harmonization drive, and in those other projects linked to it, fell by the wayside. In spite of pressures from the Commission in the form of pointed reminders that the common basis for the assessment of the VAT was connected both to the timetable for 'own resources' financing and to the EMU project, Brussels' continual calls for movement and demonstrations of 'political will' went unheeded.[21] Consequently, the beginning of financing from 'own resources' was moved back from 1975 to 1976 to 1978 and finally to 1979 when eight of the nine member-states were finally able to remit proportions of VAT receipts to Brussels. Germany had great difficulty getting the Sixth Directive assimilated into national law and thus was not prepared to fully participate in the Community's self-financing system until 1980. The EMU project fizzled for reasons having little to do with failures in fiscal harmonization.[22] None the less, the progress toward the abolition of tax frontiers envisaged under the EMU scheme did not materialize. In fact, the compromises that had to be made to save the Sixth Directive will make the future abolition of fiscal frontiers very difficult since the Nine ultimately agreed that a 'common basis' for VAT assessment need not actually mean that similar goods and services need to be taxed in every member-country.[23]

Summing up the fiscal harmonization drive in a 1980 report, the Commission foresaw 'even more serious difficulties' ahead as it contemplated pushing forward toward the standardization of VAT rates.[24] 'Such approximation,' the report continued, 'will be possible only at a much more advanced stage of economic integration.' Still, in the Commission's view, further fiscal harmonization remains 'absolutely necessary.'[25] In light of past experience, there is a reasonable probability that fiscal harmonization will progress in the years ahead, albeit very slowly.

Patterns and Puzzles

Before the concluding sentence of the last section slips by too quickly, we might like to ask what it is about 'past experience' that suggests 'that fiscal harmonization will progress in the years ahead?' Accomplishments to date have not been spectacular, but they have been consistent, cumulative and on the whole integrative. To be sure, the process described in this chapter went on for twenty-one years: it took fourteen years to create the Community VAT, and another seven to arrive at a list of items to be commonly assessed. The process was fraught with delays. Three years elapsed, 1962–65, between the Commission's proposal for a Community VAT and the Council's acceptance of the notion. Then another two years passed, 1966–67, before the Council could agree on the Directives that would actually establish a VAT. Five years, 1968–73, then went by before the new tax was in operation in all of the six original member-states, and then another seven years were taken up in efforts to standardize bases.

Yet, despite the snail's pace, fiscal harmonization in fact progressed. A common turnover tax was agreed, adopted and established; a formula for a common base was ultimately worked out. These measures contributed to eliminating trade distortions on the common market as it was intended that they would. Moreover, midway into establishing their common tax, the EC member-governments agreed to use some of its receipts to help the Community toward financial autonomy. This was also accomplished, and as a result an international authority is currently effectively taxing subjects within sovereign states. Thus, as we step back to gain some perspective on the fiscal harmonization process, the most general pattern that appears is one of slow but definite integrative movement. As suggested in Chapter 1, this pattern needs to be explained, because understanding it could contribute to our more general understanding of international collaboration and integration. Therefore, as we move into the case study materials, it will be important to discover why the Six and later the Nine were able to reach the agreements they ultimately reached. Why could they periodically make decisions and formulate policies that pushed fiscal harmonization forward and thereby furthered European Integration? What conditioned these moves? What initiated them? What consummated them?

But, then, why also was the road toward greater integration so rough? Why were there so many delays? What explains the snail's pace? After all, from the very beginning the new tax was conceived as a set of similar national taxes, so that neither national sovereignty nor national taxing prerogatives were ever infringed. Moreover, fiscal experts throughout the Community agreed that the VAT was an appropriate first

step toward harmonization, and they urged their governments to take it. Later, all agreed that establishing a common
base for assessment was a reasonable and necessary next step,
not only for fiscal harmonization *per se*, but also for the
furtherance of the 'own resources' scheme and the EMU
project. These ideas were endorsed at two Summits! Out-
wardly at least, it would seem that there was comparatively
little horsetrading or politiking among the member-
governments or between them and the Commission during
most of the long VAT experience. There was some of this, as
in the tug-of-war between Brussels and Rome over the Italian
postponements, yet not enough to lend credence to conventional explanations about slow movement because of imperatives to protect national sovereignty, or because of clashing
and incompatible national interests or inter-state contests
of power. Nor, for once, are we able to attribute even the
early problems of fiscal harmonization to the French or to
Charles de Gaulle, since the French attitude was relatively
benign throughout the VAT episode. In fact, problems
between and among countries seemed to have comparatively
little to do with the periodic stalling of the harmonization
process.

The explanation for the stalling seems instead to lie *within* the member-states. From the materials presented in this
chapter it appears that deadlocks in Brussels were not really
diplomatic deadlocks in the customary sense, but rather
periods of inactivity, mostly in the Council of Ministers,
caused by the inability of one or more of the member-
goverments to move toward positions espoused by the
majority of their partners. As long as certain governments
could not move, and as long as the unanimity rule prevailed,
debates were largely futile. For example, the Commission had
its first VAT proposals ready in 1962, but meaningful discussions about fiscal harmonization could not get started in the
Council of Ministers until the West German Government was
ready to take a definite position. This was not possible, for
West German domestic reasons, until 1964. In the same way,
even though the First and Second VAT Directives were
before the Council of Ministers in 1965, they could not be
adopted until the Dutch Government could approve them.

This was not possible, for Dutch domestic reasons, until 1967. Similarly, though the VAT was to be established throughout the EEC by 1970, it could not be put in place completely until the Italian Government could implement it, and this was not possible, for Italian domestic reasons, until 1973. In the last instance, the Sixth Directive establishing a common basis for assessing the VAT might have been acted upon by the Council as early as 1973, but it could not be adopted until British positions could be reconciled with those of the Commission and the other member-governments. This did not happen until 1977, and even then, as it turned out, the Community position had to be adjusted to suit London's needs. For domestic reasons the British Government was simply unable to modify its stance.

The pattern of periodic stalling at the Community level because of deadlock at the national level is not difficult to discern. But what remain puzzling are the causes of the domestic deadlocks. What were the 'domestic reasons' that injected rigidities into governments' stances in Community councils? What accounted for governments being *unable* to make or change policies? What determined how long governments had to remain obdurate at the Community level? When and why could governments finally abandon their inflexible positions? If domestic blockages explain characteristic stalling during the EC policy process, as the VAT episodes suggest, answers to these whats, whens and whys might explain a good deal about the course, tempo and timing of the international collaborative and integrative processes.

The third general pattern discernible in the history of the VAT experience is the combination of the first two, the shifting back and forth of discussions and debates between the Brussels arena and the domestic arenas of the different member-states. In Chapter 1 this pattern was called *political reverberation*. However, at this point it is no longer necessary to illustrate reverberation with abstract metaphors like eleven-ring circuses or progressive ping-pong. The main political contests surrounding the creation of the EEC's Value Added Tax shifted from Brussels to Bonn, back to Brussels, to The Hague and back again to Brussels. Political activities related to the implementation of the VAT in accord with the First and Second Directives shifted from Brussels to the member-countries, and in the Italian case back and forth between Brussels and Rome several times. With regard to the Sixth Directive, the main political contest moved from Brussels to London, and back to Brussels. In each of these episodes outcomes in each arena became starting points for activity in others, though many of the intermediate outcomes were of the 'no movement at all' variety which immediately shifted issues back to the arenas in which they were last thrashed about. Once the pattern of political reverberation is identified it becomes clear that EC policy-making activity in the fiscal harmonization field was continuous over the twenty-one years recorded in this study. There were delays in Community decision-making, but no pauses in the politiking that was the essence of the policy process. Long stretches of inactivity in Brussels suggested only that during these times the political action had shifted elsewhere.

In the next several chapters the general patterns identified here will be somewhat obscured as analysis focuses on particular periods of time, countries and events. The object of analysis in these more detailed chapters will be to answer the 'what, when, how and why' questions about progress and delay in EC policy-making that this chapter raised. But it will be clear by the time Chapters 3, 4, 5 and 6 are finished that they are but pieces of a large jigsaw puzzle. When fitted together in Chapter 7, they will again reveal general integrative movement paced by slow-moving governments acting in overlapping and interdependent political arenas. The ultimate picture that emerges, however, ought to be a good deal more sophisticated than the preliminary sketch offered in this chapter.

Notes

1. D. C. Kruse, *Monetary Integration in Western Europe: EMU, EMS and Beyond*, London, Butterworths, 1980, p. 7.
2. Ibid., pp. 25–9.
3. *Treaty Establishing the European Economic Community*, London, HMSO, 1973, pp. 39–40.
4. Decision of 21 April 1970, *Official Journal of the European Communities* (hereafter cited as *OJ*), L94 of 28 April 1970.

5. *OJ*, C28 of 27 March 1971.
6. Alan A. Tait, *Value Added Tax*, London, McGraw-Hill, 1972, pp. 144–64. This fourth factor also created major difficulties later when the United Kingdom introduced the VAT in the context of its accession to the EC. See Chapter 7 below.
7. For the flavor of the Italian position on this point, see E. Tamburo and C. Rivand, *Le implicazione politico-economiche e technico-amministrative della imposta sul valora aggiunto in Italia*, Rome, Istituto per l'economia europea, 1968, *passim*.
8. *European Documents*, IV/5285/59.
9. Andrew J. Taussig, 'The Impact of the European Communities Upon German Ministries,' unpublished doctoral thesis, Harvard University, 1971, p. 164.
10. Ibid., p. 165.
11. Ibid., pp. 164–6.
12. *The EEC Reports on Tax Harmonization: The Report of the Fiscal and Financial Committee and the Reports of the Sub-groups A, B, and C*, Amsterdam, International Bureau of Fiscal Documentation, 1963. The official version of the Neumark Report was published in 1962, *Bericht des Steuer—und Finanazausschusses*, Brussels, Europische Wirtschaftsgemeinschaft Kommission, 1962.
13. IV/KOM(62) 217 final. Taussig's commentary is also useful. See in particular, pp. 179–80.
14. 'Harmonizing Taxes—an Unsolved Problem; Ministerial Caution Subdues the Commission's Impetuosity,' *Common Market*, Vol. 4, No. 5 (May 1964), pp. 91ff.
15. *Agence Europe*, 30 June 1965; Taussig, op. cit., p. 194.
16. *OJ*, Spec. Ed., 1967, pp. 14–16.
17. *Agence Europe*, 10 September 1969; *Agence Europe*, 15 September 1969; 'Belgium's Export Tax Challenged,' *European Community*, No. 153, (February 1972), p. 5.
18. Actually unofficial murmurings about possible Italian delays were heard as early as 1968. See, *Agence Europe*, 16 October 1968; *Agence Europe*, 6 August 1969.
19. *Agence Europe*, 18 September 1969.
20. Donald J. Puchala, 'Domestic Politics and Regional Harmonization in the European Communities' *World Politics*, Vol. 27, No. 4 (July 1975, pp. 504–6.
21. *Agence Europe*, 26 July 1975; *Agence Europe*, 22 November 1975.
22. Kruse, op. cit., pp. 200–66.
23. *The Economist*, 16 October 1976, p. 69.
24. Commission of the European Communities, *Bulletin of the European Communities*, Supplement 1/80, 'Report on the Scope for

Convergence of Tax Systems in the Community,' Brussels, EEC, March, 1980, p. 8.
25. Ibid., p. 8.

3
West Germany and the Community VAT

In April 1967, in compliance with the First and Second Directives of the European Communities concerning the Value Added Tax, the West German Bundestag passed into law a bill creating a West German VAT.[1] West Germans began paying the new tax on 1 January 1968. Notably, this was two years ahead of the European Community's deadline for implementing this first step toward fiscal harmonization, and it was ahead of all the other member-states, except France which had had a Value Added Tax since 1954. For its expeditiousness Germany was praised as the *Musterschuler* or model schoolboy of European Integration. Compliments were also earned by a number of prominent Germans whose efforts and energies significantly influenced the creation of the Community-wide VAT. Hans von der Groeben, the EEC Commissioner who led the fiscal harmonization drive, had been a leading EEC enthusiast in the West German Economics Ministry before going to Brussels. Fritz Neumark, the West German fiscal expert and professor at the University of Frankfurt, chaired the distinguished advisory committee that recommended the VAT to the European Commission. Arved Deringer, CDU delegate, and Rapporteur for the Finance Committee of the European Parliament, led a pro-VAT chorus in Strasbourg. Rolf Dahlgrün, the West German Finance Minister after 1963 vigorously pushed the VAT in the EEC Council of Ministers.

Realistically speaking, however, very little of the conspicuous interest in the EEC tax on value added that the West German Government displayed can be attributed to 'Europeanness.' Naturally, the Federal Republic was committed to the Treaty of Rome and therefore was obligated to co-operate in fiscal harmonization. In addition, many of the individual Germans involved in the VAT drive saw themselves promoting European Integration. But, as far as the Bonn Government was primarily concerned, particularly after the summer of 1963, promoting the Value Added Tax in the European Communities was tantamount to accomplishing a major fiscal reform *in the Federal Republic of Germany*. This was why the EEC's VAT was so crucially important to the Germans. In effect, the success or failure of the reform effort in the Federal Republic, and the political rewards or penalties that would follow from changing the German tax system, came to be largely contingent upon what happened to the VAT in Brussels.

Fiscal Reform in West Germany

During the first years of the newly-established Federal Republic of Germany fiscal policies contributed notably to the recovery and rapid growth of the West German economy.[2] Germans were heavily taxed, because 'the money was needed for a variety of subsidies to support one or another of the activities favored by the State,' and West German economic success in the early post-war years 'flowed in large part, from the success of the German authorities in collecting tax revenue and their stubbornness in maintaining high tax rates.'[3] Yet, at the same time, the levying of taxes came to be highly selective, as all manner of tax incentives, deductions, credits and allowances were used to spur investment and to nurture favored sectors and industries.[4] One result of the selective nature of the fiscal system, particularly in the realm of direct taxes on incomes and profits, was a compounding inequality in the tax burden. As the tax base narrowed because of reductions and exemptions in favored sectors, and as needs for public revenue increased, rates necessarily had to be raised in the less-than-favored sectors. By the early 1950s high rates on income and corporation taxes were proving to be disincentives to investment and therefore brakes on economic growth.[5]

Recognizing the need for reform in the West German tax structure, the Ministry of Finance, in June 1953, asked its Academic Advisory Council to examine the system as a whole and to recommend ways in which it could be modified to meet the financial needs of the Government and still remain compatible with the growing economy. Later that year the Academic Advisory Council produced a report entitled *Organic Tax Reform*, where it recommended that income and corporation taxes be lowered and spread more evenly to eliminate their disincentive effects.[6] Notably, the report also recommended that the Federal Government should rely more forthrightly upon indirect taxes to meet its revenue requirements and that to accomplish this it should introduce a comprehensive Value Added Tax.[7]

At this point broader West German concerns with organic tax reform converged with more specific problems having to do with turnover taxation in the country. The Advisory Council's call for a Value Added Tax was at the same time an invitation to abolish the turnover tax then in effect in the Federal Republic. This tax, the *Umsatzsteuer*, dated from the last days of the Second Reich where it was introduced to help pay to fight World War I. It taxed the sales values of all goods and services exchanged in Germany. Though first imposed at a modest rate of 0.5 percent, the *Umsatzsteuer* was increased over the years along with the increased revenue needs of successive German governments. It was raised to 4 percent in 1951 and stood at that rate until 1966. Its yield in the mid-1960s accounted for about 30 percent of the Federal Government's revenues, thus making it a centrally important fiscal instrument.[8]

But there were problems with the *Umsatzsteuer* that were offsetting its value as a mainstay revenue producer. Most of these followed from the fact that the *Umsatzsteuer* was a 'cascade' or cumulative tax 'levied afresh at every stage in the production and distribution chain,' so that 'from one stage to the next the selling price [was] increased not only by the operator's margin but also by the amount of tax he [had] paid.'[9] In other words, the *Umsatzsteuer* taxed taxes already paid as raw materials were purchased to make products and as these products were transferred through wholesale and retail stages. As long as the rate of the sales tax remained modest, its tax-on-tax character was not particularly distorting. But with rates set at 4 percent the cumulative nature of the sales tax became quite inflationary and markedly distorted relationships between true economic value and selling price. Moreover, to the extent that it was fully shifted forward to consumers, the cascade tax had also become increasingly regressive.

The cascading German sales tax also affected competition because it encouraged the vertical integration of firms. Since taxes had to be paid at each stage of production when smaller firms exchanged semi-finished products, there was great incentive to enlarge firms so that numerous production stages would be encompassed in the activities of single fiscal units. The *Umsatzsteuer*, then, offered a boon to large-scale enterprises and definitely disadvantaged small and medium-sized firms. In fact, smaller firms were frequently unable to shift previously paid turnover taxes forward because doing so would have raised their prices to non-competitive levels. In addition, because of differences in turnover tax liabilities for different-sized firms, comparable products might have different amounts of forward-shifted taxes included in their final selling price. Therefore, there could be no reliable way to calculate the appropriate amounts of tax rebates to be returned to exporters when the products crossed international borders. Nor was there any exact way to tax imports to make them comparable to domestically-produced goods. The West German Government met these problems as best it could by imposing 'average' taxes on imports and similarly rebating 'average' tax contents on exports. Some experts concluded, however, that such average adjustments were too low by amounts sufficient to affect West German international competitiveness.[10] This disturbed German business-men, and it was naturally a matter of concern to the Bonn Government.

Finally, by the early 1950s the *Umsatzsteuer* was rapidly losing its comprehensiveness because its initially broad base had been whittled down over the years by special concessions and exemptions awarded to particular groups for social and political reasons. 'Necessities', such as some foods, were taxed at lower rates and the list of such items lengthened over time: public welfare and utilities were tax-free; agricul-tural products were awarded lower rates, as was most of the wholesale trade. Not only was the general tax beginning to look like a selective tax, but, more importantly, maintaining revenue was coming to mean higher and higher rates on those transactions that remained subject to the full tax. Some experts believed that by the early 1950s the rates of the *Umsatzsteuer* were nearing upper limits beyond which public acceptance and market distortions would become major concerns.[11]

The West German fiscal system, then, was in a certain amount of disarray as the new Federal Republic moved through its first decade. Pressures for reform were mounting: by 1954 two special commissions, the Finance Ministry's Advisory Council and the Troelger group appointed by the Bundesrat, had both recommended sweeping changes, including the replacement of the *Umsatzsteuer* with a Value Added Tax. Other academic groups were similarly advocating revisions of tax laws, and the Financial Research Institute at Cologne went so far as to prepare a draft for a law instituting a VAT.[12] Meanwhile, the Bundestag was pressing the Government to offer a design for general tax reform, while special interests, and particularly small businessmen, exporters and import-affected manufacturers, were ganging up against the *Umsatzsteuer*.[13]

The Politics of Delay

The point that must not be lost amidst this discussion of the technicalities of German taxes is that the German Government was facing pressures for fiscal reform for at least a decade before the European Commission decided upon a VAT for the EEC. Whether or not to institute a Value Added Tax, then, was a German problem before it became an EEC problem, and, in Germany, this was only a part of the larger problem of what to do about the *Umsatzsteuer*. This, in turn, was but one element of the issue of organic tax reform. To German authorities during the 1950s all of these domestic matters were more pressing, and indeed much more important, than anything having to do with harmonizing taxes internationally.

But for almost a decade after the Advisory Council's 1953

call for sweeping reform, the Bonn Government did very little to resolve the problems of Germany's tax structure. Instead, it initiated successive studies. At the request of the Bundestag in 1956 the Government re-examined the workings of the *Umsatzsteuer*; in 1959 a Technical Commission appointed by the Ministry of Finance examined the feasibility of alternative plans for tax reform; a 'Turnover Tax Working Group' set up in 1959 compared possible results of adjusting the *Umsatzsteuer* with those that would follow from instituting a Value Added Tax; in 1960 the Academic Advisory Council reviewed the turnover tax situation one more time.[14] Except for the 'Turnover Tax Working Group,' or Hartmann Commission, which came down strongly for a VAT and offered a draft law, most of the other studies reached indefinite conclusions, thus leaving final decisions to the Government. However, no decisions emerged.

Instead of acting on tax reform, the Government issued repeated statements affirming and reaffirming the need for it and its commitment to it. For example, Finance Minister Franz Etzel listed tax reform among the top priorities of the Government formed after the 1957 elections. Chancellor Adenauer sent a similar message to the Bundestag in 1958.[15] The Minister of Finance went before the Bundestag in 1961 still affirming the goal of tax reform and expressing the hope that, 'the next legislative session can take a definitive decision for the long term.'[16] Despite the rhetoric, however, the only actions concerning turnover taxation coming from the Government at this time were proposals for minor adjustments or *herumflicken*[17] to shore up the *Umsatzsteuer*.[18]

When, in 1961, Franz Etzel told the Bundestag that a 'definitive decision' on turnover tax reform was coming soon, he also explained that 'the situation [was] not at present ripe for a decision on the form and content of the new system.'[19] This was a cautious way of saying that the Government in 1961, and indeed during several preceding years, lacked the political capacity to take a definite stand behind a new Value Added Tax to replace the *Umsatzsteuer*. To move decisively in any direction at that time would have alienated important elements of support for the CDU/CSU regime either by raising the ire of voters directly or by offending various Ministers' clients. In this situation the political course of least resistance (i.e., the safest course) for the Bonn Government was to talk about tax reform, but to refrain from actually setting it into motion.

While there were sound reasons for changing the *Umsatz-steuer* to a Value Added Tax, and while there were a number of politically salient groups that wanted it changed, there were also powerful interests that were favored by the existing system and that therefore wanted to keep it. They pressed upon the Government to resist change. For one thing, because of the incentives toward industrial concentration contained in the *Umsatzsteuer* and the competitive advantages it passed to big companies, large, vertically-integrated enterprises looked askance at reforms that involved abolishing the cascade tax. Not only did such firms benefit competitively against smaller German producers on the home market, but they were also advantaged against many foreign producers by virtue of the fact that 'average' tax adjustments at the German border were for them often overcompensations. Similarly, wholesale traders, the important middle echelon of the distribution system, enjoyed markedly reduced tax rates under the *Umsatzsteuer*, and hence had no desire to change it. Nor did the numerous other groups who benefited under the *Umsatzsteuer* from exemptions and reduced rates on utility costs, professional services and the like. For years the *Umsatzsteuer* had been used as an instrument of social policy by assigning lighter burdens to underprivileged citizens.[20] The old cascade tax therefore had friends among West German voters, and the Government was not about to ride roughshod over them.

Equally significant politically were the negative reactions to the notion of a German Value Added Tax. Even people who had no good reason to prefer the *Umsatzsteuer* hesitated to rally to the Value Added Tax because the VAT's proponents could not demonstrate for certain that the new tax would be better than the old one. Studies conducted by the Federation of German Industry (BDI) acknowledged problems with the *Umsatzsteuer*, but they reached no consensus on an alternative system of indirect taxation, thus leaving the BDI split on the VAT question.[21] At the small business and retail trade level entrepreneurs had no great liking for the *Umsatzsteuer*, but they were equally leery about the VAT and particularly about the increased book-keeping the new tax would require.[22] Consumers' groups meanwhile feared that a new tax would inflate prices and raise the cost of living, and German public opinion generally endorsed the maxim *'alte Steuer gute Steuer, neue Steuer schlecte Steuer.'*[23]

The politicization of the tax reform issue within the German bureaucracy cemented the decade-long domestic deadlock. Conservative elements within the Ministry of Finance, including Finance Minister Fritz Schaffer from 1953 to 1957, hesitated to endorse the VAT because of concern about possible revenue shortfalls that might follow after a break in a fifty-year fiscal tradition and the introduction of an untried tax. As noted, the *Umsatzsteuer* had become a mainstay revenue earner, and the 1950s were the years of 'orderly housekeeping' in German financial policy where balanced budgets were seen as political as well as economic imperatives.[24] Under these circumstances a possible revenue shortfall was a most serious matter. At the same time, between the upper and lower echelons of the Finance Ministry there were differences of view about the feasibility of introducing and collecting a VAT. Those who would be assigned to actually executing the complex system had doubts about it. The leaders of relevant civil service associations were also wary of the extra work that would be required in gearing up for and implementing a dramatically new turnover tax system.[25] Then, when the Ministry of Finance finally determined to go ahead with a Value Added Tax despite internal squabbling, probably in late 1960 or early 1961, inter-ministerial feuding flared and added complications that further delayed the government's decision:

> The Ministry of Agriculture wanted additional relief for farmers, with the aid of a privileged system of tax deductions. The Ministry of Transport sought the exclusion of transport facilities from the full rate. The Interior Ministry feared that social security services and life insurance companies would be victimized. The Housing Ministry had similar anxieties over the building societies. In contrast to all of these, Professor Erhard reckoned that concessions to special interests would

lead to poorer business performance rather than lowered prices and therefore increase the dangers of inflation; so the Economics Ministry pressed for the new tax to be applied with conformity . . .[26]

As late as the autumn of 1962 there was no indication that the German Cabinet was prepared to act on the question of turnover tax reform in the Federal Republic. However, by this time the European Commission was prepared to act on the question of the Community-wide VAT and European fiscal harmonization. For the West German Government these two questions were to be politically interwoven for the next five years.

The German VAT and the Community VAT

Every analyst who has looked at the relationship between fiscal harmonization in the EEC and fiscal reform in the Federal Republic agrees that it was the Commission's decision to press for a Community-wide VAT which broke the German political deadlock over the replacement of the *Umsatzsteuer*.[27] This is true in two senses. First, the European Commission's VAT proposals injected an urgency into the German tax debate that had been lacking for most of the previous decade. Second, the Commission's proposals focused the German debate about alternatives to the *Umsatzsteuer*, since, after the autumn of 1962 the only feasible alternative appeared to be some sort of Value Added Tax. Having said this, it must also be emphasized that pressures from Brussels were only some of the factors that contributed to opening the way for the VAT in Germany. Exactly how important they were is difficult to assess inasmuch as different German officials were differently sensitive to European entreaties.[28] Moreover, and most important for this analysis, after the German Cabinet finally agreed upon a turnover tax reform bill for the Federal Republic in July 1963, the predominant direction of political pressures was from Bonn toward Brussels. Germany became the instigator, while the Community authorities often delayed.

Decisions in Brussels and Bonn

Events leading to the initiative of the European Commission in October 1962 were recounted in Chapter 2 and need not be repeated here. Suffice it to say that under the mandate of Article 99 of the Rome Treaty, after intensive study and extensive consultation, and upon the strong recommendation of the Neumark Committee, the European Commission recommended the phased introduction of a tax on value added in all member-states. The 1st of January 1970 was to be the European deadline. Up to this point there had been little direct connection between fiscal reform in West Germany and fiscal harmonization in the European Communities beyond the fact that a number of German experts, like Neumark, were involved in both.[29]

The European tax initiative, however, complicated the West German political process because it added the question of how to respond to the Commission to the already controversial question of what to do about the *Umsatzsteuer*. Since in late 1962 the Bonn Government was not prepared to respond definitively to either question, it chose to temporarily evade them, and thus alleviate pressures, by sending the Commission back to the drawing board. Hence, the German Government objected to the timetables contained in the Commission's VAT proposals and asked that the plan be reconsidered and offered again in revised form at a later date.

But while the Commission could be put off in this manner, the Europeans within the West German Government could not. For a number of key officials within the Foreign Ministry, the Economics Ministry, the Chancellor's Office and the Bundestag, the question of tax reform also became a question of European integration. For many, supporting integration symbolized 'good Germanness,' 'good Europeanness,' and the other varieties of goodness that Germans believed brought the Federal Republic acceptance in the eyes of partners and rallied international backing for broader German political and strategic goals. Naturally, to be against a Value Added Tax for Germany could now be interpreted as rejecting Europe and all the rest of the 'goods.' Suddenly, the professors, government tax experts, parliamentary deputies and interest group leaders who had been pushing for a Value Added Tax in Germany for more than a decade found new allies among the German Europeans. The domestic balance of political power therefore began to shift.

Almost at the same time, the anti-reform opposition of German big business also began to moderate, but for reasons having little to do with Europeanness. Economic conditions in Germany, and indeed in the world more generally, changed significantly around 1960, and these changes raised questions in business circles about the continuing worth of the *Umsatz-steuer*. Between 1948 and 1955 the Federal Republic developed into a world industrial center, and this was at least partly the consequence of rather severe internal contraints on consumption plus lavish encouragements to investors. While helping to create the 'economic miracle' these policies also produced strong pressures for the revaluation of the Deutschmark, and with massive surpluses of foreign exchange accumulating, a brisk inflation in the Federal Republic also threatened. Fear of inflation usually provokes strong actions from the Bonn Government. In this instance the Federal Government moved to meet the inflationary challenge with a revaluation of the Deutschmark in 1961. The move was generally successful. But, coming as it did in the wake of the French devaluation of 1958, its second-round impact was to flood the West German domestic market with imports and thus threaten the internal and external operations of some major German industries.

The reflex action in West Germany at this point was to engineer a surrogate devaluation of the DM by raising the import equalization taxes and increasing the export rebates that were parts of the *Umsatzsteuer* system.[30] But when the Federal Government proposed to do this, Germany's trading partners delivered heated protests. The United States Government recalled to Bonn that such actions were questionable under the GATT accords, and other EEC member-states as well as the Commission reminded the Germans that manipulating border taxes contradicted the spirit and letter of the Rome Treaty and contravened the Standstill Agreement of 1960.[31] The opaque nature of the *Umsatzsteuer* weakened

the West German case considerably as no one could be persuaded that the Federal Government was simply 'bringing
border taxes up to permissible levels.' Eventually, Germany
raised its border taxes despite its partners' displeasure.[32]
But as a result of the dispute both the German Government
and the businesses that were being aided by the tax adjustments concluded that future fiddlings with the *Umsatzsteuer*
at the border could be prohibitively costly over the broader
range of West German foreign relations. Therefore, the
Government and large industry would henceforth seek
another device for surrogate devaluation, and with its
potentially higher nominal rate, the VAT seemed suited for
the purpose.[33] Large industries accordingly relaxed their
opposition to the new tax.

While all of this was going on, a round of studies, including
the second report of the Academic Advisory Council,
deflated civil service objections about the administrative
feasibility of a Value Added Tax. The studies also somewhat
reassured treasury officials about the VAT's revenue
potential. Such worries were to reappear in later Bundestag
deliberations. But, by 1962 VAT proponents had at least
developed a credible case.

With opposition reasonably quelled, and with proddings
from Brussels and new support from Europeans within
Germany, the West German Cabinet was finally able to agree
on the text of a bill replacing the *Umsatzsteuer* with a Value
Added Tax. In its July 1963 proposal to the Bundestag
entitled 'Blueprint for a Turnover Tax' the Government
opted for an 'income' type VAT based on the accounts
method of calculation.[34] The VAT Bill appeared on the
Bundestag's legislative calendar for a first reading in February
1964. On 5 February it was referred to the Bundestag
Finance Committee where it was to remain for the next
three years.

Germany Takes the Community Lead

Placing the VAT Bill before the Bundestag opened a new
phase in the German debate over tax reform. In many ways
this new phase resembled what had gone before except that
Bundestag deputies now became the targets of pressure:

groups lined up on either side of the VAT issue; taxmen worried about revenues; civil servants grumbled about administrative complexities; small businessmen protested bookkeeping requirements; consumers' groups condemned regressive and price-inflating effects; special interests queued for concessions and exemptions. The Bundestag debates were not particularly partisan, though the Social Democratic Party hammered at the VAT's regressive nature and fought for special considerations for essential goods. Against all of this the Government and VAT proponents in the Bundestag offered two arguments, the first being that the *Umsatzsteuer* was seriously flawed and therefore had to be replaced. The second was that the European Communities were going to have a Value Added Tax in any event, and the Federal Republic was therefore obligated to institute one for European reasons. Here it must be borne in mind that the German Government cared a good deal more about tax reform in Germany than about tax harmonization in the Common Market. But the EEC 'imperative' offered Bonn a convenient ram to batter down its domestic opposition.

For this battering ram tactic to be effective, however, there actually had to be an *EEC imperative*! There was none in 1964: the Commission was still 'back at the drawing board' where the West Germans, and a number of other members had dispatched it after it offered its first Community VAT proposals. One reason for the Commission's withdrawal was that almost every member-state had found something to disapprove of in its original proposals and these objections had to be sorted through the EEC's consultative mechanisms in order to find compromises and arrive at appropriate revisions.[35] The consultative process was necessarily lengthy. But, even more importantly, to move the fiscal harmonization process forward the Commission needed at least one strong ally from among the member-governments. Somebody had to want a Community-wide VAT badly enough to push it through the Council of Ministers, and this was something that the Commission by itself was clearly unable to do. At this point the Commission's needs for an ally and the West German Government's needs for a political battering ram coincided exactly. For domestic reasons Bonn

needed some forceful directives from Brussels telling member-
states that they must institute the Value Added Tax. For
Community reasons the Commission needed to persuade the
Council of Ministers to adopt its directives.

The West German Government therefore tried to get the
EEC to tell it to do something that it badly wanted to do in
any event. Bonn, consequently, moved to lead the drive for
a Community VAT. The symbolic impact of having the
economically most powerful member state behind the
harmonization drive was important in itself. Beyond the symbolism, there was also action. Concerted German prodding
in EEC deliberations was discernible in several Community
forums from the autumn of 1963 onwards. In the European
Parliament, German delegates urged the Commission to get
on with the revisions of its initial VAT proposals.[36] At
meetings of the Council of Ministers German representatives
pressed first for the acceptance of the principle of a
Community VAT and then later for the approval of the
Directives that established the new tax.[37] First results of
these efforts were registered at the meeting of Finance
Ministers in Rome in February 1964, where near agreement
was attained on the principle of a Community-wide VAT.[38]
This was reaffirmed at the Luxembourg meeting in April
1964, where 'a strong pact [was] visible between the German
Finance Minister and the responsible Commissioner Hans
von der Groeben.'[39] These meetings opened the way for
renewed discussion of the Commission's proposals which
were ready in revised form in June 1964. Since by this time
Brussels clearly understood the contingency between the
Community VAT and the German VAT, the revised proposals specifically omitted all that the West German Government had found objectionable the first time around and
included a timetable tailored to the German liking.

But the Commission's proposals of June 1964 were vague,
particularly with regard to the form that the VAT was to
take, the base or 'basket of goods and services' to which it
was to be applied and the reductions and exemptions that it
would allow. This vague form was unhelpful to VAT proponents in West Germany because it equipped opposition
elements there with reasons for delaying the parliamentary

process. 'We cannot move until Brussels clarifies its preferences,' was an easy excuse for inaction. Furthermore, any
differences that might emerge between the Community
Directives and the German VAT Bill would invite questions
and prompt time-consuming digressions into technical
detail. Similarly, Community indefiniteness was keeping alive
the hopes of German special interests for exemptions, and
this was encouraging a relentless assault on the Bundestag
Finance Committee. In light of this, the Germans pushed
hard in Brussels to move the Commission along from their
general proposals to much more specific Directives. The
Bundestag Finance Committee, for example, called for
specificity from Brussels in a resolution tabled in October
1964; German deputies supporting the VAT issued a similar
appeal to the Commission in November; German representatives in the COREPER pressed the Commission again in
December 1964 and through the winter of 1965.[40]

The European Commission finally set the detailed drafts
for the First and Second VAT Directives before the Council
of Ministers in the spring of 1965. While compatible in most
respects, the draft Directives differed from the German Bill
in some important ways. In particular, the Commission proposed a consumption type Value Added Tax calculated by
the 'invoice' method, because it felt that such a tax would
most readily lead to the abolition of fiscal frontiers in the
EEC. This differed from the German Bill's 'income' type
tax calculated by the account method. In addition, the Commission's version differed from the German Bill in the treatment of capital goods and agriculture. Rather than open the
way to opponents' questions about these differences between
Brussels and Bonn, and thus prompt further parliamentary
delays, the Bundestag Finance Committee adjusted the
German Bill to bring it closer to the EEC drafts.[41]

By the end of 1965 all that was needed at the Community
level was affirmation by the Council of Ministers. This was
also really all that was needed to bring debate in the German
Bundestag to a close and to get the German VAT Bill passed
into law. In the course of the German debate most of the
traditionalist affinity for the Umsatzsteuer had been undermined. What was left was probably silenced in 1966 when the

Umsatzsteuer yielded its first ever decline in revenue. Almost at the same time the Federal Constitutional Court handed down a decision questioning the compatibility between the *Umsatzsteuer* and the Basic Law of the Federal Republic.[42] Then, the formation of the Grand CDU/CSU/SPD Coalition Government in December 1966 effectively removed any lingering partisanship from the tax issue. Thus, with domestic contentions fading and with their Value Added Tax nearly ready to be put into place, the Germans were prepared to be 'model Europeans.'

Yet, despite German prodding and no little anxiety, the VAT Directives were tied up in the Council of Ministers for most of 1965 and 1966 for reasons that had nothing to do with the internal affairs of the Federal Republic. The Dutch Government had erected obstacles to the adoption of the Community VAT that will be discussed at length in the next chapter. Once these were removed in the early winter of 1967 events in both Brussels and Bonn moved rapidly. In February 1967, the Council of Ministers agreed in principle on the texts of the First and Second Community VAT Directives.[43] Almost immediately, in March 1967, the Bundestag Finance Committee released the German VAT Bill, which, not surprisingly, called for a Value Added Tax for West Germany that looked almost exactly like the tax called for in the EEC Directives. Then, on 1 April 1967 the Council of Ministers formally adopted the VAT Directives. On 26 April the German VAT Bill was passed by the Bundestag. It became law in the Federal Republic in June 1967, thus making West Germany the first EEC member-state to formally comply with the new Community Directives, and thus also making the West Germans the *Musterschulern* of European integration.

West Germany and the Politics of Fiscal Harmonization

Of course the West Germans were able to comply so readily with the EEC Directives because of the interdependence of Bonn's and Brussels' VAT designs. Collaboration between German and Community officials over several years produced a set of Directives that asked the Federal Republic to do just exactly what it wanted to do, i.e., reform its turnover tax system. The West Germans could then be 'good Europeans' during the early phases of the Community's fiscal harmonization largely because tactical considerations in their domestic politics invited such a pro-EEC stance. By asking Bonn to do what it wanted to do anyway, the European Commission's prodding enhanced the political capacity of the German Government and strengthened it in its contests against domestic opponents of tax reform. The 'Europeanization' of the reform issue in Germany lent the proponents of domestic tax reform valuable allies and compelling arguments.

Meanwhile, because Bonn was able to give early support to the European harmonization effort, the Commission's political capacity was also enhanced. As a rule, the Commission commands a modicum of authority because of its technical expertise, and it is sometimes able to exert influence over member-governments when it searches out compromises and bridges divergent national positions. But it wields very little political clout in its own right, and it is usually unable by itself to move member-governments away from obstructionist positions. To do this it needs support from Community members. This is precisely what the West German Government provided between 1964 and 1967. Thus the marriage of interests between Brussels and Bonn solved political problems for both. These observations on the West German experience will take on added significance in later chapters where reverse dynamics are revealed in instances where particular member-governments and the Commission find it impossible to support each other, much to their mutual frustration.[44]

Brussels and Bonn not only influenced the outcomes of each others' policy-making processes, but also their respective tempos. For the Germans, the period of Community involvement in their turnover tax reform, from 1962 to 1967, was actually a latter phase of a domestic political contest over the *Umsatzsteuer* that began before 1953. But until 1962 the German decisional process, because of the controversy that surrounded it, was moving so slowly that one analyst called it a 'permanent tax reform.'[45] The Commission's call for a Community VAT, however, changed the political context of the German tax reform, added some urgency, altered the balance of political forces, and speeded the Cabinet toward endorsing a Value Added Tax for Germany. This German decision, in turn, speeded the Community process which, because it lacked national support, was in abeyance in the fall of 1963 and the winter of 1964. German leadership and a Bonn–Brussels coalition effectively accelerated the Community policy process through most of 1964. But then the indecisiveness of the Commission and a deadlock in the Council of Ministers again stalled the policy process at the Community level, and this, in turn, affected the process at the German domestic level. The Bundestag Finance Committee would not report out the German VAT Bill until the terms of the European tax were clear and until its adoption was assured. The VAT issue consequently bounced back and forth, or 'reverberated,' between Brussels and Bonn as outcomes in each political arena either stimulated activity or prompted inactivity in the other. Actors in each arena moved as fast or as slowly as outcomes in the other permitted.

While the Bonn–Brussels minuet proceeded, most of the other Community members watched and waited. After some early encouragement from the Gemans, all of the other governments, save for the Dutch, accepted first the idea of Community-wide VAT and then the terms and formulas set forth in the First and Second VAT Directives. The Dutch held out for quite some time, and this disturbed the German Government as the next chapter explains. Nevertheless, there was very little politiking among governments at the Community level during the first phase of the European fiscal harmonization process. Little government-to-government bargaining occurred, little international posturing, little threatening and little pushing except for some nudging on the Dutch within the COREPER.[46] Instead, the most heated contest was *within West Germany*, and domestic outcomes in the Federal Republic determined and paced the movement of European policy-making. This pattern was to be repeated several more times as fiscal harmonization inched forward.

Notes

1. This chapter draws extensively on materials previously published in Donald J. Puchala and Carl Lankowski, 'The Politics of Fiscal Harmonization in the European Communities,' *Journal of Common Market Studies*, Vol. 15, No. 3 (March 1977), pp. 155–79. Lankowski did the interviewing in West Germany and most of the analysis of German texts.

2. Andrew Shonfield, *Modern Capitalism: The Changing Balance of Public and Private Power*, New York and London, Oxford University Press, 1965, pp. 266–7.

3. Ibid., pp. 266–7.

4. Ibid., p. 296.

5. Malcolm Maclennan, Murray Forsyth and Geoffrey Denton, *Economic Planning and Policies in Britain, France and Germany*, New York, Praeger, 1968, pp. 190–3.

6. Wissenschaftlicher Beirat beim Bundesministerium der Finanzen, *Organische Steuerreform*, Bonn, 1953. Cf. also, Maclennan, *et al.*, pp. 190–1.

7. Gunter Schmölders, *Turnover Taxes*, Amsterdam, International Bureau of Fiscal Documentation, 1966, p. 54.

8. Manfred Schrim, 'The Value-Added Tax in Germany' in *The Value-Added Tax: The U.K. Position and the European Experience*, T. M. Rybczynski (ed.), Oxford, Basil Blackwell, 1969, p. 30.

9. Schmölders, op. cit., p. 32.

10. Organization for International Cooperation and Development [hereafter cited as OECD], *Report on Tax Adjustments Applied to Exports and Imports in OECD Member Countries*, Paris, OECD, 1968, p. 48.

11. Schmölders, op. cit., pp. 36–43. The untidyness of the *Umsatzsteuer*, due to complicated exemptions and concessions, was criticized in the so-called *Troelger Report* commissioned by the Bundesrat in 1952. See, *Diskussionsbeitrage des Arbeitsausschusses für die Grosse Steuerreform* (Ein Bericht an den Finanzausschuss des Bundesrats) herausgegeben von Dr. Jur. Heinrich Troelger, 1954, p. 85.

12. Finanzwissenschaftliches Forschungsinstitut an der Universität Köln, *Entewurf eines Gesetzes zur Änderung des Umsatzsteuergestzes nebst Bergündung*, Cologne, 1953.

13. Schmölders, op. cit., p. 55; Manfred Schrim, op. cit., p. 31; Dieter Pohmer, 'Germany' in *The Value Added Tax: Lessons from Europe*, Henry J. Aaron (ed.), Washington D.C., The Brookings Institution, 1981, p. 91; Andrew J. Taussig, 'The Impact of the

European Communities Upon German Ministries,' unpublished doctoral thesis, Harvard University, 1971.

14. *Denkschrift über die Möglichkeit einer Verbesserung der Umsatzsteuerrung*, 1958: *Zur technischen Durchführung der Umsatzsteuer-Reformvorschläge*, 1960; *Studie zu einer Mehrwertsteuer mit Vorsteuerabzug*, 1960; *Problem einer Nettoumsatzbesteuerung*, 1960.

15. Taussig, op. cit., p. 157.

16. Ibid., p. 160.

17. 'Patches'.

18. Cf., *Denkschrift über die Änderung des Umsatzsteuergesetzes*, Deutscher Bundestag, 2. Wahlperiode, 1953, Drucksache 1924; Deutsch Bundestag, Drucksache 730, op. cit.; Schmölders, op. cit., pp. 55–6; Taussig, op. cit., p. 160. There was, however, a partial income tax reform in 1958.

19. *Frankfurter Allgemeine Zeitung*, 3 July 1961.

20. Cf., *Troelger Report*, op. cit., p. 85.

21. Bundesverband der Deutschen Industrie, *Entwurf eines Umsatzsteuergesetzes mit Durchführungsbestimmungen und Begründung*, Heft 1 und 2, 1957, Heft 3, 1958; Cf. also, Puchala and Lankowski, op. cit., p. 163; Gerhard Braunthal, *The Federation of German Industry in Politics*, Ithaca, N.Y., Cornell University Press, 1965, pp. 257–63.

22. Pohmer, op. cit., p. 93.

23. 'Old tax good tax, new tax bad tax.'

24. Andrew Shonfield, op. cit., pp. 272–5; 283–5.

25. Taussig, op. cit., p. 184.

26. Ibid., pp. 183–4.

27. Cf., Schmölders, op. cit., p. 56; Pohmer, op. cit., p. 92; Schrim, op. cit., p. 32; Taussig, op. cit., pp. 182–6.

28. This was apparent in our interviews, where it appeared that pressures and perspectives from Brussels were most attended to in the Bundestag and the German Foreign Ministry, and least acknowledged in the Ministry of Finance.

29. *Frankfurter Rundschau*, 17 June 1963.

30. Technically this was called the *Umsatzaugleichsteuer* or 'turnover equalization tax.'

31. Robert Baldwin, *Nontariff Distortions of International Trade*, Washington, The Brookings Institution, 1970, pp. 84–9.

32. *Novelle Umsatzsteuergesetz*, 4 June 1963.

33. Because of its cascade nature the *Umsatzsteuer* could not be imposed at rates much higher than 4 percent without becoming unduly regressive and highly inflationary, whereas a VAT, because of its net nature, could be imposed at considerably higher rates.

34. The technicalities of calculating and collecting Value Added Taxes are largely irrelevant to this analysis. However, at this point it is important to note that the German Cabinet proposed an 'accounts' method tax. This was later modified by the Bundestag Finance Committee in deference to the European Community. See below p. 57.

35. See, Chapter 2, p. 31-2 for the different governments' objections.

36. *European Documents*, 121/1962-63, No. 56, 20 August 1963.

37. Much of this activity makes up the subject matter of Chapter 4 because West Germany (and after a time almost everyone else) was pressing on the Dutch. See, pp. 76-7.

38. Only the Dutch demurred at this point.

39. Taussig, op. cit., p. 169.

40. Puchala and Lankowski, op. cit., p. 12; Taussig, op. cit., p. 189.

41. Pohmer, op. cit., p. 92. Actually, the differences over the treatment of agriculture were never reconciled because political conditions in the Federal Republic would not permit this.

42. Schrim, op. cit., p. 32; Pohmer, op. cit., p. 91.

43. See, Chapter 4, pp. 79-80.

44. See, Chapters 4 and 6 in particular.

45. Maclennan, *et al.*, op. cit., p. 193.

46. Scc, Chapter 4, pp. 76-7.

4

The Dutch interlude

Someday, when the archives of the European Council of Ministers are opened to scholarly scrutiny, the documents will reveal that the meeting of Ministers of Finance on 9 February 1967 resulted in a compromise that removed the last major obstacle in the way of the First and Second VAT Directives.[1] The compromise was between the French and Dutch governments, and more precisely between French Finance Minister Michel Debré and Dutch Prime Minister Jelle Zijlstra.[2] Their agreement concerned some apparently technical points contained in Article 17 of the Second VAT Directive. On balance it favored the Dutch. But the French, and the other member-governments, understood that this bowing to the Dutch position was the political price that had to be paid for the cooperation of the Netherlands in the launching of the Community-wide VAT. The passing of Dutch resistance in the winter of 1967 ended a standoff in the European Community that had held up fiscal harmonization for nearly two years.

Readers will recall that the West German Government was prepared in principle to move toward a Value Added Tax as early as 1964. France was also willing to go forward at this time, and Belgium, Luxembourg and Italy had joined the consensus by the autumn of 1964. Moreover, by the spring of 1965 West Germany, for all of the reasons explained in Chapter 3, was anxious to bring EEC deliberations concerning the VAT Directives to a rapid close. Drafts of the First and Second Directives were before the Council of Ministers and VAT proponents in the West German Bundestag were waiting for the EEC to put its texts into final form so that the German VAT Bill could also be put into final form. They also awaited final EEC passage so that once and for all German domestic opponents could be silenced with a *fait accompli*. But the Council of Ministers was unable to act on the VAT Directives during the last half of 1965, throughout 1966 and into the winter of 1967. The problem was that according to the Treaty of Rome the Council's decision to initiate fiscal harmonization had to be unanimous, and unanimity could not be secured as long as the Dutch Government opposed the Value Added Tax. Thus, much to the dismay of the West Germans and to the consternation of all others involved, the Dutch held firm, one against five, month after month, and effectively forced the first phase of fiscal harmonization to a standstill.

The obstructionist stance of the Dutch Government during this VAT episode was highly uncharacteristic: most of the time, the Dutch are stalwart supporters of European integration and leaders in harmonizing efforts. This makes the Dutch resistance to the Community VAT all the more interesting to try to explain. Moreover, since, as this chapter will show, the roots of this 'uncharacteristic' Dutch behavior were in the domestic politics of the Netherlands, the episode nicely illustrates the linkage between political contests at the national level and outcomes at the Community level. More often than not, the play of Dutch politics yields national positions that support EEC initiatives and cast Dutch statesmen in 'good European' roles. Naturally it would be revealing to ask and answer why this is generally the case. But, what is more to the point here is that the play of domestic politics can also *deny* statesmen the 'good European' role—even in Holland. How, when and why this can come about are the central concerns of this chapter.

As it turns out, there are really two 'why' questions that need to be answered about Dutch behavior with regard to the Value Added Tax between 1964 and 1967. First, we must learn why the Dutch Government initially and stubbornly rejected the EEC's VAT. What was it about the proposed new tax that was so onerous to the Dutch that they chose to stand alone against their five partners for two years? There must have been some compelling reasons behind their negative stance. However, if this was the case, then the second question is all the more challenging: why did the

Dutch Government reverse its stance in 1967? What brought about the change of policy that permitted Prime Minister Zijlstra to ultimately entertain a compromise? It was not the technical points yielded by the French in February 1967 that altered the Dutch stance. These were in the nature of rewards to the Dutch for having already reversed their position. Beforehand, something had obviously happened in The Hague which allowed Dr Zijlstra to accept a compromise in Brussels. What had happened and why?

The Official Argument Against the VAT

In October 1962, the Dutch Government answered the European Commission's first proposals for a Community-wide Value Added Tax with an emphatic 'no.'[3] But since most of the other member governments also voiced reservations at that time, the distinctiveness and firmness of the Dutch position were not yet discernible. However, when the other governments yielded to the Commission's reasoning (and West German prodding) between 1963 and 1964, the Dutch did not. The Netherlands could not join in the Community consensus, the Dutch Government explained, because they could not accept the idea of beginning the process of European fiscal harmonization by instituting a common turnover tax. At least they could not accept this idea until they could better understand its broader implications for the Netherlands and for the European Common Market. To gain such an understanding, Dutch officials told their Community colleagues they needed more information from the Commission. What the Dutch asked for was the blueprint for the Commission's ultimate scheme for Community-wide fiscal harmonization.[4] Was the EEC moving toward the abolition of fiscal frontiers where Community taxes would be so standardized as to obviate any and all adjustments at national borders? Or, was the Commission not planning to push fiscal harmonization this far? Was the Commission perhaps aspiring instead only to neutralize the distorting impacts of indirect taxes on intra-Community trade? Did the Commission have a supplemental plan for the harmonization of excises and direct taxes, or was it not thinking this far ahead? Where, in short, was the proposed VAT to fit, and what role was it to play within the overall context of the European Community's fiscal evolution?

Moreover, Dutch officials went on to explain that these concerns about overall designs were not merely demands for intellectual neatness. Answers to the Government's questions would have a practical bearing on the fate of the existing cascade-type turnover tax already in force in the Netherlands. If the VAT were to be introduced, the existing tax would have to be dismantled, and this was not to be taken lightly since most Dutch fiscal and financial authorities believed that the existing tax ideally served a variety of Dutch economic and social-political purposes.[5] As a matter of fact, ever since the European Community struck upon the idea of a Value Added Tax in 1960, Dutch fiscal experts had been finding fault with it by arguing that it compared unfavorably with the existing turnover tax in the Netherlands.[6] The experts reasoned that the Netherlands had the best system of indirect taxation in the world, and there was thus no reason to reform it. In light of this, the Dutch Government officially contended that it could not exchange a fiscal instrument of known efficacy for an untried one unless it could be persuaded that moving to the VAT was genuinely a step toward European integration—and a correct one! It could not be thus persuaded until it examined and assessed the full blueprint for fiscal harmonization in the EEC.

The official Dutch case against the principle of a VAT as a first harmonizing step was written into a memorandum to the European Commission sent in the early summer of 1964, wherein the Commission was asked:

to pass an opinion, indicating the pros and cons, as to whether the undertakings to be made in the proposed Directive should be based on the broad concept of suppressing fiscal barriers, or on the more confined principle of neutrality of turnover taxes when it comes to the origin of goods and services rendered.[7]

To this the Commission quickly responded in August 1964 with a lengthy memorandum to the Council of Ministers arguing that whether or not to begin fiscal harmonization by instituting a common turnover tax was really a null question since the Treaty of Rome stipulated that harmonization should commence in this area. As to the ultimate goals of fiscal harmonization, the Commission indicated that 'there has never been any doubt about the scope and objectives to be fulfilled by the harmonization of turnover taxes, as called for in Article 99 of the Treaty.'[8] The scope, in the Commission's interpretation, included the total abolition of fiscal frontiers, and the objective was fiscal harmonization as an element of complete economic and monetary union. The harmonization of excises and direct taxes would come in due time as these too were elements of higher-level economic integration.

Despite the Commission's reasoned and apparently convincing answers to the Dutch questions, and in spite of the assurances about ultimate integrative goals that they contained, there was no outward evidence of any change in the Dutch position during 1965 and 1966. Indeed, there was little indication that the Dutch Government had even considered the Commission's response. As late as November 1966, *Agence Europe* was still reporting that 'all delegations have confirmed the agreement of the member states with the adoption of a joint tax on value added, except the Dutch delegation, which maintained a general reservation.'[9]

Smokescreens and Background Noises

There are two reasons why the dialogue between the Commission and the Dutch Government concerning the principles of fiscal harmonization and the place of the Value Added Tax failed to move the Dutch. First, the Dutch Government's public concern about principles, plans and blueprints was not its only concern about the VAT. Indeed, the publicly-voiced Dutch opposition to the new tax was but the tip of an iceberg of political resistance that blocked any change of policy. Second, the Commission's response to the Dutch inquiry about the future course of fiscal harmonization was not entirely welcomed by the Dutch Government. Instead of comforting the Dutch with the promise of progress toward European integration, the Commission's assurances about the eventual attainment of complete fiscal harmonization raised anxieties in The Hague and fortified the positions of Dutch opponents of the VAT.

The extent to which the Netherlands' 'principled objections' to the VAT were facades remains unclear. Some Dutchmen undoubtedly attributed significance to the case made about principles, and most of those in the Government and among interest groups and political party elites interviewed in 1977 believed that the Government was justified in pushing the Commission to clarify its designs of European fiscal harmonization. On the other hand, most of those interviewed who were closest to the policy-making process in The Hague recalled that the official protests about the incompleteness of the Commission's fiscal designs were voiced primarily as a smokescreen to cover more fundamental reasons for coolness toward the proposed Value Added Tax.[10] In effect, the Dutch Government preserved face and stalled for time by raising issues of high principle, while it simultaneously grappled with pressures and internal dissensions that were sapping its ability to be more cooperative in Brussels.

For one thing, Dutch businessmen from small and medium-sized firms ran a vigorous anti-VAT campaign from 1962 onward under the auspices of their trade association, the *Raad Voor Het Midden-en Kleinbedrijf*.[11] The large business community in the Netherlands was also opposed to the VAT, but, according to Dutch officials their campaign was mounted too late to affect the policy debate within the Government. The main concern of the smaller firms was the probability that the new turnover tax would be extended to the retail level and that it would therefore be levied on the transactions of all but the tiniest businesses. For the retailers and for the Netherlands this would be a new departure in taxation, since, under the turnover tax system then in effect, small businesses were completely exempted. The burden, as the small businessmen saw it, was not so much in the tax itself, which was shifted to the consumer in any event, but in the new requirements for accounting and other paperwork which would drain both time and money.[12] Wholesalers at the middle-sized firm level were also concerned with the proposed VAT because they were favored with very low rates under the existing tax which fell primarily on producers.[13] In addition, Dutch public opinion, aroused by lively media coverage, was anxious about the impacts of the proposed VAT on prices. Labor felt strongly both about preserving concessional rates for products that could be considered everyday necessities, and about preserving Holland's very progressive ratio of indirect to direct taxation.[14] However, instead of rejecting the VAT *per se*, Dutch Labor leaders pressed for concessions and compensations within the new system. Except for Labor, which directed its lobbying efforts at the political parties, most of the interest group opposition targeted the Ministry of Finance.

Anti-VAT pressures from Dutch society, however, had only marginal impacts on the Government's stand against the new tax. 'There was a lively public debate over the VAT,' one Dutch official commented, 'but it could be considered noise in the background.'[15] This was not because the Government was insensitive to public opinion, but rather because public opinion was pressing for a position that the Government was predisposed to take in any event. In this sense, the pressures from the interest groups were welcomed by the Government. But they were almost superfluous because the most implacable resistance to the VAT came from within the Government itself. The core of this internal opposition was an elite corps of Dutch fiscal officers in the Ministry of Finance clustered around the State Secretary for Finance. They perceived their influence, autonomy and wisdom, as well as Dutch national sovereignty and interest, all challenged by the EEC's movement toward fiscal harmonization.

The crux of the Dutch taxmen's concern was that abolishing fiscal frontiers in the European Communities by introducing a common Value Added Tax and then standardizing its base and rates would take a most important instrument of fiscal policy away from the national government. The Dutch fiscal officers wanted to be able to alter national turnover tax rates upwards or downwards as might be required to help moderate economic cycles. They also wanted to be able to grant tax concessions and exemptions as social needs suggested. Within the existing Dutch turnover tax system they were able to do these things, but they feared that, with harmonization, control would be transferred to Brussels (as indeed it would at some very distant stage). This was additionally troubling to the Dutch taxmen because there was little leeway left in the system of the Netherlands for using direct taxes as counter-cyclical instruments, particularly if upward adjustments were called for. Furthermore, if the rates of indirect taxation were to come under EEC control, the Common Market would be able to affect the ratio of indirect and direct taxation in the Netherlands and thereby 'interfere' in Dutch social policy by affecting fiscal progressivity.

Thus, there was the widely shared feeling in the corps of Dutch taxmen that national fiscal systems were 'forbidden domains' as far as Brussels was concerned, and, as one Dutch official explained, 'this European integration business is probably something that is all right for Agriculture, but certainly not for the Treasury.'[16] Revenue collection was perceived as the essence of national sovereignty; revenue collectors perceived themselves to be the custodians of this sovereignty. They were not prepared to relinquish their trust out of deference to 'theoretical ideas thought up by others in Brussels.'[17] Along with this reaction against outside interference went the widely-endorsed notion, noted earlier, that the existing turnover tax system in the Netherlands was the best in the world, and something much more appealing than the 'French-inspired' VAT would have to emerge before the Dutch tax would be willingly dispensed with. At the very foundations of the Finance Ministry's negative and adamantine stand were the personal attitudes of a number of individual officials, particularly those who had designed the existing Dutch cascade tax and had made their careers out of perfecting it and overseeing its application. Here, personal pride almost demanded that the proposed VAT should be found wanting.

In this anxious context, with the Dutch Finance Ministry thus on the defensive, what the European Commission believed to be calming reassurances were actually taken as threats. When the Dutch Government asked the Commission about its overall design for fiscal harmonization, about the last thing that the Ministry of Finance wanted to hear was that the bases and rates of the VAT would eventually be standardized by Community authorities. This is precisely what the Dutch taxmen feared! It amounted to the snatching away of their autonomy and the blunting of their most effective policy instrument. Paradoxically then, the Commission's attempt to overcome Dutch scepticism about the VAT by explaining how it would contribute to greater European integration had the opposite effect, at least within the Dutch Ministry of Finance, of fortifying anti-VAT opposition. Elsewhere in the Government and in Dutch society more broadly the EEC assurances had their intended effect, and support for the Community Value Added Tax was rallied on European grounds. But all this really meant was that the Community had managed to split the Dutch polity. The resulting domestic political contest remained at stalemate for the better part of three years.

What support there was for the VAT in the Netherlands was largely founded upon commitments to European integration. Dutch Europeans acquiesced in the Commission's designs for fiscal harmonization because the Treaty of Rome called for such a common policy, and the logic of intensifying economic unity required it. But, as one Dutch respondent explained, the Europeans were lukewarm about the VAT. 'We felt that the EEC had a lot to do and that it was no big thing about being held up on this issue.'[18] In Dutch society 'support' for the proposed new tax really amounted to the absence of opposition. No one was very enthusiastic except for a few academics. Within the Government, the Foreign Ministry took a rather strong stand in favor of the VAT because they were 'trying to make something of this European thing.'[19] The Ministry of Agriculture fell in with the Foreign Ministry, once it was affirmed that Dutch farmers were to be exempted from the VAT, and the Ministry of Economics joined the intra-bureaucratic proponents after econometric analyses convinced them that introducing the VAT would have little effect on Dutch prices.[20] Most Dutch parliamentarians supported the VAT for European reasons. But the parliament was not an important arena for debate on this issue because the decision on the VAT was a Cabinet prerogative.

Despite differing views among major ministries, the negative position of the Ministry of Finance was all that was needed to fix the Dutch Cabinet in a bureaucratic gridlock. During the VAT episode the apex of the policy-making apparatus that prepared the Dutch positions taken in Brussels was the Subcommittee on European Integration Affairs of the Dutch Council of Ministers. This group regularly consisted of the Prime Minister, the Foreign Minister and his State Secretary, the Finance Minister, the Economics Minister, the Minister of Social Affairs and the Minister of Agriculture. They were responsible for the instructions that guided Dutch representatives to the European Council of Ministers. Immediately subordinate to this group was the Interministerial Coordinating Committee, composed of senior civil servants from the various ministries. This committee prepared the Dutch positions for the weekly meetings of the COREPER held in Brussels. What is most noteworthy in the standard operating procedures of both the Subcommittee and the Coordinating Committee is that they tended almost always to defer to, and accept, the preferences of the ministries within whose jurisdictions particular issues were most nearly located. Fiscal harmonization and the Value Added Tax, of course, fell under the jurisdiction of the Ministry of Finance, and, since Finance opposed the Community tax proposals, the Coordinating Committee opposed them, the Subcommittee opposed them, and the Dutch Cabinet opposed them. Under such conditions, instructions to Dutch delegations in Brussels would therefore remain consistently negative concerning the VAT as long as the Ministry of Finance persisted in its opposition. Dutch delegates would then say 'no' in Brussels because the Finance Ministry said 'no' in The Hague.

Interestingly, the bureaucratic gridlock extended down into the Ministry of Finance as well. Deference there was accorded to experts within whose areas of competence issues most nearly fell. In the case of the VAT, the State Secretary for Finance deferred to his turnover tax experts, and the Minister of Finance deferred to his State Secretary. Consequently, as long as the experts remained opposed to the VAT, the Ministry remained opposed. As a matter of fact, a number of well-informed officials interviewed felt that in this particular case a single middle-echelon fiscal expert provided a great deal of the intellectual force and firmness behind the Ministry's anti-VAT position.

The Dutch Position Changes

Explaining the Dutch shift from opposition to cooperation in the drive toward European fiscal harmonization involves piecing together another jigsaw puzzle. In light of the analysis thus far, the simple answer to why the Dutch attitude toward the VAT changed must be that the Finance Ministry's attitude changed. This was apparently true, for, as noted in the introduction to this chapter, Finance Minister Zijlstra was able to accept a compromise on technical points in the winter of 1967. The compromise itself notwithstanding, what is significant here is that by the end of 1966 the dialogue between the Dutch and the other Five had gotten down to technical points. This is a long way from where the discussions were even a few months earlier when the Netherlands was holding out against the VAT on the basis of lofty principles. Something then had clearly moved the Dutch Government during 1966, and this implies that something must also have moved the Ministry of Finance.

As the standoff between the Netherlands and the EEC stretched from months to years, a variety of pressures accumulated and intensified. Political temperatures in the issue area rose noticeably as Europeans and VAT proponents both within and outside the Dutch Government grew impatient. At Cabinet meetings and in lower-echelon interministerial forums in The Hague the Foreign Ministry stepped up efforts to convert the reluctant taxmen to Europeanism. Agriculture joined this effort. Some dissension apparently also developed within the Finance Ministry where some officials wavered to the point of exhibiting willingness to at least consider alternatives to the existing turnover tax system. From outside the Government some of the larger export-oriented Dutch firms began to grow anxious about what might happen to them competitively if the European Communities implemented the VAT without Dutch

participation. Concurrently, some of the other EC governments began to hint that the Five could well go on without
the Netherlands and that the political will to do just this was
building.[21] Germany pressed the hardest, and at one point
Finance Minister Strauss warned that the 'value added tax
was no less urgent for Germany than were common agricultural prices for Holland.'[22] Thus, the issue of the Dutch
delay was clearly heating up.

Dutch delegates were put under considerable pressure
within the EEC institutions. During the period of stalemate
technical work on the Community-wide Value Added Tax
continued in various Brussels forums including the Standing
Committee of Heads of National Revenue Departments and
the COREPER. The aim of the Brussels authorities and the
other five governments in these EEC working groups was to
pressure the Dutch by isolating them and by emphasizing
the unreasonableness of their position in the light of the
strong consensus in the opposite direction. It was hoped that
the Dutch delegates would be persuaded and then convert
their home-office colleagues. 'The message we wanted the
Dutch delegates to take home,' one Community official
explained, 'was how can you be right against all of the other
members?'[23]

In the vocabulary of EC bureaucratic politics, applying
pressure by isolating and unanimously opposing uncooperative governments is rather colorfully referred to as 'flushing
down the W.C.'. This technique, Community officials agreed,
is often 'very, very effective.' As one described it:

> Here is a case of placing a man in a group of peers and demonstrating
> to him that his peers stand uniformly against him. In a national govern-
> ment a single man can hold up legislation indefinitely if he happens to
> be the man in authority in a particular area. Nobody can overrule him
> because he is top man. However, when set against men from other
> governments that are his counterparts or peers he cannot argue from
> a position of unapproachable authority; he has to argue a case strictly
> on its merits and to make his position carry he has to persuade others
> of its rectitude. After trying, and failing, he must back off or lose
> credibility. This is called 'flushing down the W.C.'.[24]

If a recalcitrant national government maintains its positions despite such peer pressuring in EC inter-governmental

committees, Community officials or other governments may ultimately choose to elevate the contentious issue—still unresolved—into the Council of Ministers, thus setting the stage for a political showdown. At the Council level the political stakes are raised. Proceedings are nearer to public view and political losers risk embarrassment and possible electoral sanctions in their countries. At the same time, the winners risk alienating the losers, thus making future co-operation more difficult. Moreover, whenever there must be winners and losers in EEC political contests the continuing unity of the Common Market system is jeopardized. As a rule then, political showdowns in the Council of Ministers are avoided, and the Dutch holdout over the VAT never really produced one. But in the autumn of 1966 many in the Commission and in the Council Secretariat perceived that frustrations over the long Dutch delay were driving the Six toward some sort of high political denouement. One Community official said of fiscal harmonization at this point that a confrontation in the Council of Ministers 'would either cap it, or kill it.'[25]

Officially, the Dutch opposition to the Value Added Tax was relaxed in the late autumn of 1966 because intensive studies and long-range projections had convinced the Ministry of Finance that existing taxes could not satisfy the future revenue needs of the Dutch Government. Income taxes were already very high and could not be raised very much more without severely dampening economic activity. At the same time the existing turnover tax could not be raised without seriously affecting the competitiveness of Dutch exports, since under the cascade system it was all but impossible to completely neutralize the tax content of exported goods. A VAT applied over a broad base, that was fully transparent and could be raised without affecting export prices, would therefore admirably meet the Dutch Government's future needs. Officially then, upon soberly rethinking the situation, the Dutch taxmen changed their minds, and this cleared the way for a compromise in Brussels.

Undoubtedly, by the autumn of 1966 some Dutch fiscal officers had been converted, partly by the pressures from outside, and partly because the VAT would indeed solve anticipated revenue problems. However, most of the taxmen were not converted. This was particularly true of those clustered immediately around the State Secretary for Finance who had stood firmly against the VAT from the beginning and who had stiffened in opposition as the pressures were applied. What actually happened was that these Finance officials eventually lost the intra-bureaucratic contest in The Hague.

Decisive encounters in the Interministerial Coordinating Committee and the Subcommittee on European Integration Affairs apparently occurred between November 1966 and January 1967. In October 1966, the government of Dutch Prime Minister Cals fell. This Government had been in office throughout the VAT episode, as had Finance Minister Dr Ir. A. Vondeling who firmly supported his State Secretary and senior civil servants in their opposition to the Value Added Tax. In mid-November, after a few weeks of maneuvering, Jelle Zijlstra formed a new coalition Cabinet that was to be a caretaker regime which would remain in office until the general elections scheduled for February 1967. Zijlstra, a professor of economics and former finance minister, assumed the obligations of both Prime Minister and Minister of Finance in the new government. The State Secretary for Finance was removed, thus greatly reducing the political clout of the anti-VAT faction in the Finance Ministry. No new State Secretary was appointed.

During December 1966 Prime Minister Zijlstra was persuaded by his own analysis of the fiscal implications of the VAT, by the arguments of his colleagues in the Foreign Ministry and by other Europeans, and by hints that the Five might actually move without the Netherlands, that the Dutch Government should abandon its opposition in Brussels. Zijlstra then moved at the Cabinet level to overrule the VAT opponents in the Ministry of Finance. 'They never dropped their opposition,' a European Community official reported. 'He simply overruled his own technical advisers. It was a political decision.'[26] Zijlstra's dramatic move ended the long play of VAT politics in the Dutch arena.

The Compromise in Brussels

Dr Zijlstra arrived at the 9 February 1967 meeting of the European Council of Ministers prepared to compromise on the issue of the Community Value Added Tax. The five-against-one political showdown would therefore be averted, face would be saved, and the First and Second VAT Directives would finally be shaped for adoption later in the spring. But problems remained with regard to the draft of the Second Directive. This draft set down in detail how the Value Added Tax would be implemented in EC member-states. At issue, particularly between the Dutch and the French, was the question of whether national governments could offer exemptions from the VAT and whether they would be permitted to tax some transactions at a 'zero rate.' The French called for the tightest regime possible and argued that exemptions and zero rates would upset the logic and smooth functioning of the system of assessments and rebates that was the genius of the value added form of taxation. For their part, the Dutch wanted the loosest regime possible so that national governments could retain maximum flexibility in using the turnover tax as an instrument of fiscal and social policy. Whether an approved VAT would emerge from the 9 February Council meeting depended upon the extent to which the Dutch and French Governments could reconcile their differences.

The issues were technical, to be sure. But their importance is amplified when they are put in political context. Dr Zijlstra had just overruled his senior civil servants in The Hague and had probably exhausted a considerable measure of political capital in doing so. What is more, he had upset Dutch bureaucratic convention by refusing to defer to authority based upon jurisdiction and expertise. He therefore undoubtedly had some political fences to mend and some confidences to rebuild. This made it imperative that he should return from Brussels with some rewards to distribute among his disgruntled and harshly-treated fiscal advisers. As one Community official phrased it, 'he had to take something home with him' from Brussels.[27]

Significantly, what Dr Zijlstra went after, and got, in

Brussels was much of the national flexibility in the application of the turnover tax that the Dutch taxmen feared would
be snatched away from them by the European Communities.
This fear, it will be recalled, was at the heart of the Finance
Ministry's opposition to the Community VAT. The French
initially balked at the untidy tax that would follow from the
Dutch proposals, but Finance Minister Debré finally offered
to go along with exemptions and zero rates for a 'transitional
period.' Definitive Community action on the application of
the VAT was thus postponed in the interests of compromise
and unanimity.[28] Dr Zijlstra accepted the French offer, and
the compromise was drafted into the amazingly ambiguous
wording of Article 17 of the Second Directive on Fiscal
Harmonization.[29] The Dutch interlude was over.

The Netherlands and the Politics of Fiscal Harmonization

The most obvious conclusion to be drawn from this Dutch
experience with European fiscal harmonization is that the
imperatives of European integration created issues in Dutch
domestic politics that might otherwise never have been
raised. Reforming the turnover tax system was certainly not
something that the Dutch wanted to debate about in their
country. Yet, they were compelled by their participation in
the European Communities and their commitments to
regional partners to do precisely what they wanted to avoid
—i.e., to fight among themselves about taxes. Moreover,
they were compelled to contest this issue (that they did not
want to contest at all) along lines that had little to do with
conventional cleavages in Dutch politics. VAT proponents
took their stand largely on European grounds; opponents
perceived themselves protecting national interest and
autonomy. There was really no Left, Center and Right in
this, nor any Confessionalism or Anti-Clericalism. The
political dividing lines were drawn not by Dutch political
tradition, but rather by the outside world. The extent to
which participation in the European Communities can affect
a national political agenda was muted in the West German
case examined in Chapter 3. There, tax reform was already
on the agenda before the EEC took its initiatives, and politics

during the West German episode were contested along rather conventional lines of economic interest. But this was clearly not so in the Dutch case where the domestic arena was invaded and politiking somewhat distorted by 'alien' issues. We will see that much the same thing happened in the Italian case examined in Chapter 5.

European institutions were active and quite partisan in the Dutch case. The Commission and the Secretariat of the Council of Ministers orchestrated Brussels' efforts to move the Dutch Government by using the continual meetings of negotiating bodies and coordinating committees to apply pressure. Through the multi-leveled structure of EC committees, the Community gained access to national officials in various bureaucratic ranks. Consequently, it was able to intervene in national debates that were going on in several ministerial and inter-ministerial forums. By scheduling meeting after meeting on the VAT question the Brussels authorities helped to keep the intra-bureaucratic debate going in The Hague. Since Dutch delegates needed to be instructed, the occasion of each meeting in Brussels raised questions in The Hague about what the instructions ought to be. This forced those Dutch officials who wanted to continue the standoff to re-explain their position to their colleagues, and frequently to defend and re-defend it before doubters. Dutch delegates also had to explain themselves anew at each Brussels' meeting, to listen to others counter-arguments, and then to return for further instructions for the next scheduled meetings. In this sense, the EC system has a certain capacity for 'wearing down' opposition from recalcitrant governments.

In the Dutch case, however, the results of such wearing down, via pressuring, isolating, 'flushing' and the like tended to be mixed. The Community's pressure tactics probably contributed to, but did not actually cause the Dutch change of position. To try to wear down national opposition is usually a slow, tedious and ultimately uncertain tactic, and Brussels can in the end be only as effective as it is patient and persuasive. Even then, much still depends upon whether a reluctant member-government is amenable to persuasion at all. Neither Community organs nor Community officials can easily compel an uncooperative government to do anything it does not want to do. This is not a question of formal authority, which EC institutions often possess under the Rome Treaty, but really a matter of political clout built upon a base of power.[30] Dutch finance officials undoubtedly experienced some discomfort while they held out against the entire EC system. But they could have held out much longer, and probably would have if the political shake-up in The Hague had not occurred. The Community then is not without political instruments, and neither is it reluctant to use them. But these are of limited effectiveness and will not normally determine outcomes in tests of political tenacity.

The political dynamics of the Council of Ministers, however, are more determinative. As the stalemate dragged on, it became increasingly clear that the Five were not going to let the Netherlands block fiscal harmonization indefinitely. For the West Germans especially, the domestic costs of delaying the VAT were escalating rapidly. Chapter 3 explained why. Technically speaking, the Dutch were entitled to cast their veto again and again, since the Treaty of Rome stipulated that decisions about Community-wide turnover taxes had to be unanimous. Politically, however, the Five could and would do as their interests dictated, and the Netherlands therefore faced the risk of a five-to-one *fait accompli* executed in the Council of Ministers. The Five might have gone on without Holland. The risk of such a power play was greater because the Netherlands was in fact the Netherlands—i.e., a small country in a large trading system, and a country much more dependent than depended upon. Had the Five actually implemented the VAT without the Netherlands, the costs to the Dutch would have been a good deal greater than the costs to most of the others. This lesson in comparative power was not lost on Dr Zijlstra. Unanimity requirements in EC decision-making are intended to protect national interests. But, in practice, they protect the interests of the larger countries more reliably than those of the smaller ones.

It must be underlined that Dutch uncooperativeness between 1964 and 1967 was not a matter of faltering *political will*, as this was defined in Chapter 1. Dutch pronouncements repeatedly reaffirmed the Netherlands' commitments to European Integration, the country's fealty to the Rome Treaty and the Government's endorsement of fiscal harmonization as an integral part of economic union. In the light of the Netherlands' consistent and enthusiastic support for the EEC system, before the VAT episode and since, and the Dutch reputation for 'good Europeanness,' there is no reason to doubt the sincerity of these affirmations. Indeed, the Dutch Government wanted to cooperate with EEC partners during the VAT episode, and it would have if it could have.

The Dutch resistance to Value Added Tax rather resulted from *political incapacity*. The Dutch Government did not cooperate with Community partners because, under prevailing domestic political conditions, it could not cooperate. Politically, the situation in the Dutch Cabinet from 1964 to 1967 was similar to that which prevailed in the West German Cabinet during 1961 and 1963. Debate was lively. But no one could or would muster the political force necessary to break the stalemate because the domestic costs of putting down the anti-VAT opposition were perceived to be greater than those incurred in continuing the standoff. No one in the Dutch Cabinet chose to directly take on the Minister of Finance or to challenge his powerful State Secretary on the VAT issue. What, after all, would have been gained in Dutch politics by doing this? Pushing for a VAT would certainly have earned little favor among Dutch interest elites, or among most voters of whatever persuasion. Nor did most Cabinet members feel that it was worth risking coalitional unity on an issue such as the Value Added Tax. All of this dictated inaction in the Cabinet, and this rendered the Dutch Government incapable of cooperating with their EEC partners for an extended period of time. No one ever did directly take on the Minister of Finance or his State Secretary. They were toppled when the governing coalition came apart in November 1966, and the Dutch Government's political capacity for cooperation on the VAT issue in the EEC increased only after the Government itself changed.

Notes

1. This chapter incorporates data and arguments earlier published in my piece 'European Fiscal Harmonization: Politics During the Dutch Interlude,' in *Contemporary Perspectives on European Integration*, Leon Hurwitz (ed.), Westport, Conn., Greenwood Press, 1980, pp. 209-24.
2. At this time Dr Zijlstra was also serving as Minister of Finance.
3. Andrew J. Taussig, 'The Impact of European Communities Upon German Ministries,' unpublished doctoral thesis, Harvard University, 1971, pp. 177-80.
4. *Agence Europe*, 8 November 1966.
5. K. V. Antal, 'Harmonization of Turnover Taxes in the Common Market,' *Common Market Law Review*, Vol. 1, No. 1, June 1963, pp. 41-57.
6. C. P. Tuk, 'Onze verbruiksbelastingen bij internationale samenwerking,' *Weekblad voor fiscaal recht* (May 1960), pp. 399ff; C. P. Tuk, 'Verleden, heden en toekomst van de omzetbelasting,' *Weekblad voor fiscaal recht* (February 1961), pp. 30ff.
7. *Europe Documents*, No. 335, 9 September 1965.
8. Ibid., p. 1.
9. *Agence Europe*, 8 November 1966.
10. Interviews conducted in The Hague, 6, 10 and 11 January 1977.
11. Raad Voor Het Midden-en Kleinbedrijf, *E.E.G. en emzetbelasting*, 's-Gravenhage, 1963; *E.E.G. en emzetbelasting II*, 1965.
12. Raad Voor Het Midden-en Kleinbedrijf, 1965, op. cit., pp. 49-56.
13. Taussig, op. cit., p. 176.
14. Interview, Amsterdam, 14 January 1977.
15. Interview, The Hague, 13 January 1977.
16. Interview, The Hague, 10 January 1977.
17. Ibid.
18. Interview, The Hague, 10 January 1977.
19. Interview, The Hague, 11 January 1977.
20. Interview, Rotterdam, 20 January 1977.
21. Interview, Rotterdam, 20 January 1977.
22. Taussig, op. cit., p. 194.
23. Interview, Brussels, 17 January 1977.
24. Interview, Brussels, 17 January 1977.
25. Interview, Brussels, 17 January 1977.
26. Interview, Brussels, 17 January 1977.
27. Interview, Brussels, 17 January 1977; Cf. also, *Agence Europe*, 9 February 1967, pp. 4-5.
28. The issues of exemptions and zero rates returned to haunt Com-

munity policy-making in the context of the Sixth VAT Directive. See, Chapter 6 below.

29. European Communities, 'Deuxième Directive du Conseil du li
    avril 1967,' *Journal Officiel Des Communautés Européennes*,
    14 April 1967, pp. 1303/67–1312/67.

30. This point is illustrated even more dramatically in the Italian case
    discussed in Chapter 5. Here there was no question about the locus
    of formal authority, yet the Community institutions still lacked
    real political power.

5

Italy postpones the VAT

None of the national experiences examined in this book more clearly illustrate the difference between political will and political capacity than the case of Italy and the Community VAT.[1] Though Italian taxmen voiced some early doubts about being able to collect the complex new Value Added Tax, there was never any real question about Rome's desire to cooperate in the EEC's drive toward fiscal harmonization. Treasury Minister Tremelloni announced Italy's support for the fiscal harmonization effort and the Community-wide VAT at the meeting of EEC Finance Ministers in Rome in February 1964.[2] Successive Italian governments maintained this position through 1965, 1966 and 1967, and Italy joined its EEC partners in pledging to implement the First and Second VAT Directives by 1970. Yet, despite Rome's good intentions it none the less took three additional EEC Directives—two of them specifically addressed to Italy—and three years beyond the 1970 deadline to finally establish a Value Added Tax in Italy.

The novel aspect of the Italian struggle to implement the VAT is that it occurred *after* the EEC Council of Ministers had formally decided to go ahead with fiscal harmonization. Unlike the West German and Dutch episodes, where the countries' problems affected the substance and timing of the Community's decision-making, the Italian case had to do with enforcing an already decided EC policy. Examining this case therefore illuminates some of the problems of enforcement in the European Communities.[3]

On the other hand, the Italian experience with the VAT is also strikingly similar to the West German and the Dutch ones in that the sources of the Italian Government's difficulties with the EEC were essentially domestic and fundamentally political. In the Italian case, however, the issue of the Value Added Tax was politicized domestically after, rather than before, the Government had made a commitment to the European Community. Throughout the episode, from late 1967 to the beginning of 1973, the Italian Government found itself politically wedged between a strong domestic opposition to the VAT on one side, and some impatient EEC partners plus the European Commission on the other. Interestingly, the Dutch, who had only a short time before extricated themselves from the jaws of a similar political vice, led the protest against the Italian-invoked delay.[4] They were joined by the West Germans whose hopes to quickly implement the Community VAT were once again frustrated.

Why, then, was the Italian Government unable to set a Value Added Tax into operation by 1 January 1970? Of course, 'domestic politics' is the ready answer. But, why was the VAT issue so widely and intensely politicized? Moreover, why in particular did the Italian Government encounter political difficulties only after the first two VAT Directives had already been adopted? How and when did the Italian Government deal with its political dilemmas, and why did it select the particular course of action that it actually pursued? When did it become possible for Italy to implement the Value Added Tax? What ultimately made this possible?

Italy Delays

Officially, the Italian decision to postpone the introduction of the Value Added Tax was related to the complexity of the fiscal reforms that would have to take place to make room for the VAT.[5] Italian officials explained that because of the sweeping changes that would have to take place to accommodate the VAT in the country's already complicated tax structure, the process of implementation was going to take longer in Italy than elsewhere.[6] In fact, the VAT was to be a part of a much broader reform of both indirect and direct taxation in Italy, and in Rome's thinking the reform had to be an all-or-nothing exercise since changing some taxes while leaving others was impractical. The VAT was to replace the prevailing cascade-type turnover tax, the *Imposta Generale Sull'Entrata* (IGE), plus a number of other indirect taxes then being levied either on certain goods or services or within certain localities. In this way, the new VAT would greatly simplify the indirect tax system. However, if introducing the VAT were not accompanied by a complementary income tax reform, the overall effect could be highly regressive and therefore politically unpalatable. This is because the VAT would have to be introduced at a considerably higher rate than the IGE in order to bring in a comparable amount of revenue, since it was replacing not only the IGE but a number of other sales taxes as well. If a new, stiffer turnover tax were combined with existing income taxes a substantial increase in the Italian tax burden would be the result. Hence, income taxes had to be reduced, and tax reform in Italy had to be a package that could not be undone. Shaping this package, Italian officials explained, was going to take some time.

The fiscal reform process was already underway in Italy in the mid-1960s while the VAT was being discussed in Brussels. But it was moving at snail's pace primarily because neither the Italian Cabinet nor the Parliament wanted to cope with the political problems that would assuredly result when altered taxes shifted burdens among classes, interests and factions in Italian society. When the EEC issued its VAT Directives in the spring of 1967 a note of urgency was added to the Italian tax reform effort. But little action followed.

In October 1968 the Italian Government hinted that it was encountering difficulties of a 'technical and economic' nature with regard to instituting the VAT. Finance Minister Ferrari-Aggradi suggested at this time that the deadline of 1 January 1970 was probably unrealistic and that Italy would likely require an extra two years to complete its fiscal reform and to set the VAT mechanism in place.[7] High-level Italian officials repeated this message at a meeting with EEC Commissioner von der Groeben in March 1969.[8]

Neither the Commission, nor other member-governments were pleased about Italy's apparent reneging on its commitment to implement the Value Added Tax by January 1970. After the March 1969 meeting between the Italians and Commissioner von der Groeben, the European Commission addressed a stern letter to Rome voicing grave concern about Italy's intent to ignore the VAT deadline. The Commission stressed the serious inconvenience that such a delay would cause, not only for the fiscal harmonization process, but also for the implementation of the Community's 'own resources' plan. They therefore cautioned that in the event that Italy went through with its postponement, the Council of Ministers might be asked to authorize other member-states to take action against Italian exports under Article 101 of the Rome Treaty.[9] Other member-states had been protesting for some time that the Italian tax system, and especially the IGE, favored Italian exporters and discriminated against international competitors in some key sectors by over-compensating exports and overtaxing imports. They were therefore most unhappy to learn that the Italian tax reform was not going to take place on schedule, and they encouraged the Commission's efforts to dissuade the Italian Government from going ahead with the postponement.[10] None the less, in August 1969 the Italian Government submitted to the EEC an official request for authorization to postpone the VAT for two years.[11]

Between September and December 1969 extremely complex, three-way bargaining took place among Italy, the European Commission and other member-states of the Community.[12] Italy wanted an unconditional grant of postponement for two years. But the Commission sought not to halt fiscal harmonization for more than one year. It also asked that Italy's Value Added Tax be in an advanced form when finally implemented, that Italy pledge itself to the total abolition of fiscal frontiers by a specified time and that the Italian Government take steps during the period of postponement to eliminate trade distortions effected by manipulations of the IGE at Italy's borders.[13] Other member-governments meanwhile encouraged the Commission to stand firm against Italy. For their part, the Italians accused these other governments of duplicity and suggested that they look after their own trading practices. The three-cornered debate heated as the autumn of 1969 wore on. For example:

—In answer to Italy's request for postponement, EEC Commissioner von der Groeben insisted that 'it is essential that the Commission should be very strict in its control of the respecting of obligations by member-states and should not allow one government or another to evade the application of Community decisions.'[14]

—In response to the Commission's threat to set conditions on a grant of postponement, Italian Finance Minister Bosco indicated that the 'Italian Government cannot accept any connection between postponement of the application of the VAT and other problems relating to international trade.'[15] The Minister responded to the specific conditions proposed by the Commission by insisting that the postponement had to be for two years, that the VAT would be applied only up to the wholesale stage and not all the way to retailers as the Commission implied when it requested 'advanced form;' that the question of the complete abolition of fiscal frontiers was a different matter entirely, and that changes in the rates of compensation at the Italian frontiers during the postponement period were unacceptable.[16]

—As to the views of other member-states and the pressures they were bringing to bear on both Italy and the Commission, *Agence Europe* reported that 'in view of the repeated concern expressed in some member-states about the dynamics of Italian industry in some sectors, it is to be expected that most of the delegations will insist that Italy abandon all tax practices considered questionable.'[17]

—But, as noted, the Italians saw these protests coming from other member-governments as merely maneuvers for competitive advantage, and they chided their EEC partners for cloaking their commercial self-interests with legalistic arguments about Treaty obligations.[18] Reflecting these Italian Government views, the influential Milan daily, *Corriere Della Sera*, editorialized that:

> The formalistic rigor with which such questions are being considered in Brussels is indeed surprising and could even justify some suspicion. It seems that they want to hinder the expansion of Italian exports, not only in the Community but also and above all to third countries. This would be a rather odd way to assure, as the EEC must, the play of competition among the producers of the Common Market.[19]

On 1 October 1969 the Commission sent to the Council of Ministers a draft Directive permitting Italy to postpone the

VAT, but only under strict conditions including (1) the time limit of one year, (2) the call for advanced form upon implementation and (3) the request for the adjustment of existing Italian border taxes. This carried the debate directly into the Council where the Italian Government could be brought under maximum pressure from other member-states. But so too in the Council of Ministers could Italy still cast a veto.[20] Thus, either a stalemate or a compromise would have to emerge from the Council's deliberations. Time, however, appeared to be running somewhat against the Italian Government inasmuch as Rome would be legally delinquent and in infraction of the VAT Directives as of 1 January 1970. The Commission would then be entitled to institute proceedings against Italy that could ultimately bring a sanction from the European Court of Justice.[21] There is no evidence, however, that the Italian Government took this threat of possible legal action at all seriously. Nevertheless, as the 1 January deadline approached there was a flurry of meetings of the Council of Ministers, interspersed with high-level excursions between Rome and Brussels. These finally yielded a compromise: Italy exchanged some downward adjustments in some of its export rebates and import taxes for a two-year postponement of the VAT. The rest of the Commission's 'rigorous' conditions interestingly disappeared in the bargaining process.[22]

In April 1970 Italy informed the Commission that it had adjusted border taxes as previously agreed. But this was not the end of the Italian episode. By November 1970 the Italian Government was again hinting that implementing the VAT by the new deadline of 1 January 1972 might be impossible.[23] This was followed by a second formal request for postponement submitted to the Commission in October 1971. Another three-cornered debate ensued, though less heated than the first one. Another compromise was reached, and another postponement was granted, this time for six months to 1 July 1972. But still the episode was not over: by March 1972 yet another high-level Italian delegation was in Brussels. Though the legislation implementing the Value Added Tax had been passed by the Italian Parliament in late 1971, Rome officials told the Commission that 'technicalities' still barred the beginning of tax collections and that some more time was needed to actually get the system going.[24] There was, moreover, some reasonable reluctance on the Italians' part to introduce a new sales tax, which applied to services as well as goods, at the height of the summer tourist season. Rome therefore asked for another six months. Bargaining produced another Directive in July 1972 and the Italian VAT was put off until January 1973.[25] The tax finally came into force in Italy on New Year's Day 1973. Notably, in the course of all of the tugging and hauling over the Value Added Tax, the comprehensive Italian fiscal reform, i.e., the 'all-or-nothing package,' fell behind and then fell away altogether from its connection to the VAT. In any event, Italian implementation ended the three-year delay in the drive toward European fiscal harmonization.

Domestic Politics and Turnover Tax Reform

The Italian Government's expressed reservations about not wanting to go ahead with the Value Added Tax except in the context of more comprehensive tax reform were reasonable and genuine. It is also true that the Italian Government was not administratively prepared to collect the new tax and it possibly could have taken more than two years to bureaucratically 'tool up' for the task even if the Italian Cabinet and Parliament had produced authorizing legislation in 1968 when most of the other member-governments produced theirs. But these factors cover only part of the explanation for why the Value Added Tax had to be delayed. The more fundamental explanation for the Italian failure to move on the VAT was that the Government was very weak, opposition to turnover tax reform was very strong, and support for the VAT was almost non-existent in the Italian society and polity. Under these circumstances action in compliance with the EEC directives was perceived by the Italian Government to be politically very dangerous.

During the period 1967 to 1973 nine Italian governments rose and fell, five finance ministers came and went, and two Parliaments were elected and dissolved. Since almost any contested issue could unseat one of these fragile governments, political wisdom suggested avoiding controversy, and political survival meant retreating from anything that might cause a governmental crisis. This certainly meant softpedaling tax reform, and it particularly meant leaving the IGE alone, since this was Italy's most important tax and Italians had learned to live with it over a period of many years. As one Italian official explained, 'the whole period in Italy was one of turmoil, overheated politics, and continuing crisis. It was hardly a time to change anything, let alone the fiscal system of the country.'[26]

Explaining the weakness of the post-war Italian Government is beyond the scope of this study. Textbook writers, however, describe the Italian political system as a case of extreme fragmentation along numerous ideological, functional, religious and regional lines that frequently immobilizes the country's rather disorderly, but still legitimate and respected, domestic institutions.[27] Because of the diversity of political factions and interests in Italy, and the incompatibilities of the political extremes, building and maintaining sufficient consensus to govern is consistently difficult. At times it becomes impossible. Tenuous multi-party coalitions tend to easily unravel in the face of controversial issues. The cost of Italy's highly pluralistic democracy is a very slow-moving and frequently interrupted policy process. Most Italians, however, favor paying this cost rather than suppressing expression and debate.

Nevertheless, great caution in the face of potential or real opposition and divisiveness is a common Italian governmental response. This affected the handling of the issue of the Value Added Tax at two points in time. First, the Italian Government was reluctant to raise the VAT issue in Italy during the several years that it was being debated in Brussels. In effect, the VAT debate in Italy, or at least those aspects of it that took place outside of the Government, could not take place before the EEC Directives were adopted because the Italian Government provided interest groups, parties, factions and the general public with very little information about what an Italian VAT would or could look like and entail. This withholding of information was partly the result of uncertainty within the Government about the shape of the new tax, but, more importantly, it was the result of the Government's attempt to avoid open debate and a possible political contest or crisis over turnover tax reform. As long as the fate of the VAT was uncertain in Brussels, particularly in light of the Dutch standoff, the Italian Government considered that the issue was best left alone in Italy. Avoiding the issue in this way of course later backfired on the Italian Government because the question had to be raised when the EEC directed member-states to institute the new tax. At this point the VAT was injected into Italian politics like a bolt out of the blue! 'Difficulties could have been avoided, or at least lessened,' an Italian official recalled,

had the VAT been given more advanced publicity. No one understood really what it was all about. Nobody was told what items were to be taxed at various rates and specifically which items fell into which categories. If more understanding of the VAT had been the case, resistance might not have been so strong.[28]

When the Italian Government could no longer avoid the issue, it either had to submit to domestic pressures or be overwhelmed by them and possibly fall in a crisis. The VAT was a major issue in Italy, and almost all interests and factions were critical of the new tax, with the possible exception of the Europeans in the Foreign Ministry and in the elite of the Christian Democratic Party. Therefore, in what became almost a diametric opposite of the West German case, where the Government was pushed to favor the Community VAT, the Italian Government was domestically pressured to reject it.

Opposition to the VAT came mainly from outside the Government. Among the Italian public, objections to the new tax ranged from very general to very specific. Public opinion generally opposed the VAT out of anxieties about increased prices. The lack of public information about the tax fed rumors of very high rates and substantially increased prices, and the press helped these along with reports of price inflations in other countries where the Value Added Tax was already operating.[29] These concerns about prices, moreover, were set in the more or less traditional Italian context of resentment toward all taxes and residual distrust of almost

any government and its policies. 'Government public relations in tax matters is not very good,' an Italian finance
officer said. 'Everybody thinks that tax is unfair to him, and
everybody thinks that tax reform means tax increase.'[30]
More specific and organized protests about the anticipated
price effects of the VAT were directed by Italian consumers'
associations like the *Unione Nazionale Consumatori* which
campaigned actively against turnover tax reform.[31]

Italian businessmen, from multinational managers to
street-corner shopkeepers, were also against the VAT. While
the directors of large enterprises had no particular objections
to the Value Added Tax *per se*, they were extremely reluctant to see the IGE disappear. Like other cascade taxes, such
as the West German *Umsatzsteuer* examined in Chapter 3,
the *Imposta Generale Sull'Entrata* favored large integrated
enterprises because they were able to reduce taxes by replacing inter-firm transactions with intra-firm transfers.[32] In
addition, exporters among the large firms (which meant most
of them) benefited further from IGE rebates at the border,
which, due to the opaqueness of the tax, frequently exceeded
the amounts of taxes actually paid on the exported commodities. At the same time, imports entering Italy were also
taxed at 'average' IGE rates, which again frequently turned
out to be higher than rates which domestic traders paid on
similar items.[33] Interview respondents described the system
of tax subsidies and barriers at the Italian border as a package
of 'little gifts' to Italian industry. It was these practices
bound up with the IGE that were annoying other EEC
countries when they protested the Italian intention to postpone the VAT.[34] However, from the point of view of Italian
industry, if not having a VAT meant keeping the benefits
of the IGE, they preferred not to have a VAT.

Smaller Italian businessmen, particularly shopkeepers,
artisans and small entrepreneurs in the service industries,
had even greater problems with the idea of changing turnover taxes. They perceived the new tax as a threat to their
very livelihood. And, since Italy is largely a country of small
businessmen, their objections carried considerable political
weight. In the first place, the small entrepreneurs anticipated
greatly increased bookkeeping burdens as they tried to cope

with the intricate VAT mechanism of assessments and rebates. This, they argued, would mean time and money and it
would directly cut into their already slender profit margins.
But more importantly, small businessmen were concerned
about the invoicing required in a Value Added Tax system.
This threatened the widespread practice of non-invoice trading,
by which the IGE was frequently evaded altogether. It also
established a record of income upon which authorities might
base and collect direct taxes. The real problem with the VAT
then was that it was difficult to evade, and its bookkeeping
requirements made other taxes difficult to evade as well.[35]

The political Left in Italy also objected to the proposed
change in turnover taxes. However, their concerns were not
so much over the form of the new tax, but over its rates and
the breadth of its application. The IGE exempted food and
offered special concessions on other necessities. Leaders of
the Left, especially in the Italian Communist Party and in the
principal labor unions, wanted similar provisions in the VAT.
Otherwise, they argued, the new tax was likely to be highly
regressive and 'prejudicial to the little man.'[36] The anticipated regressive nature of the tax became an even greater
concern to the Left after 1971 when it became increasingly
clear that reforms of the income tax were not going to
accompany the VAT as originally planned. Therefore the
sales tax increase would not necessarily be moderated by
income tax reductions. As late as February 1975 the Italian
Communist Party was still pushing draft legislation in the
Chamber of Deputies that would make indirect tax reform
impossible unless accompanied by income tax reform.[37]

Rather unexpectedly, as far as Rome was concerned,
mayors and other political officials in Italian principalities
also mobilized against the VAT. Again, their concern was not
so much with the new tax itself, but with the fact that other
indirect taxes would be abolished when the VAT went into
operation. Some of these other taxes happened to provide
the main sources of revenue for many local governments.[38]
'This,' one Italian official commented, 'was not exactly to
the liking of the municipalities.'[39]

Opposition to the VAT was also present within the Italian
Government where it was mainly concentrated at the middle

echelons of the Finance Ministry. Like Dutch fiscal officers, Italian taxmen were also conservative. Their major concern was with the unpredictability of revenues under the proposed VAT.[40] The VAT was to replace the IGE, which was, after all, Italy's most important source of public revenue, and Italian finance officials had no accurate way of determining what the exact yield of the VAT would be. Nor could they accurately ascertain at what rate the VAT would have to be imposed in order to yield revenues comparable to those produced by the IGE. The issue was complicated by the fact that the extent to which the IGE was being evaded was unknown.[41] Nor could it be known how extensively the VAT would be evaded. These questions were rendered all the more important because the Italian economy was slowing at the beginning of the 1970s and tax collections were already dropping below estimates.[42] For all of these reasons Italian fiscal officers balked at turnover tax reform, or, as one respondent put it, 'they moved with feet of lead.'

The other major intra-bureaucratic objection to changing the turnover tax system came from the directors of the *Casa Per Il Mezzogiorno*, southern Italy's economic development program. To help spur development in the south the Italian Government had incorporated special exemptions into the IGE and other indirect taxes. These would apparently disappear when the VAT was set into operation, so that 'those holding exemptions were of course reluctant to give them up, and those offering these exemptions had mixed feelings about changing the system.'[43]

In the face of such strong and widespread opposition, and in the absence of almost any support on the VAT issue, the Italian Government found itself in a political dilemma. To comply with the EEC's VAT Directives, as they were obliged under the Rome Treaty, might have brought down the Italian Government. Yet continued refusal to comply meant increasing pressure from the European Commission and other EEC governments. Moreover, Italian uncooperativeness might eventually have invited EEC sanctions against the country's exporters. The Italian dilemma was assuredly also holding up progress toward European fiscal harmonization, and Rome was uncomfortable about this.

Italy Opens the Way to the VAT

Under the circumstances in which it found itself, the Italian Government did what was most appropriate: it kept the VAT issue out of the domestic arena for as long as possible, and then it bargained with the European Community for time. The bargaining occurred during the three interludes in 1969, 1971 and 1972 when the EEC was asked to grant Italy the initial postponement and the two subsequent extensions. In each instance the Commission answered Rome's request by proposing to impose rather harsh conditions in exchange for the grant of postponement. Thereupon Italy rejected the Commission's position and insisted that there be no conditions. The Commission deliberated but remained firm and the question of postponement was then put to the Council of Ministers where discussions typically started in the COREPER. Before moving the issue to its formal agenda, the Council consulted the European Parliament and awaited its report.[44] Then, each time that the matter of postponing the VAT in Italy was finally taken up by the Finance Ministers of the Six, a compromise was reached that was rather favorable to Italy and the postponement was granted. Altogether these bargaining interludes—from the time that Italy first hinted about postponement, to its formal requests, to the Commission's counter-proposals, to the Council's consultations, to the final compromises—took nearly thirty-one months.

Given its inability to act on the VAT domestically, the Italian Government naturally sought to draw out the bargaining process as long as possible. In this the European Commission was Italy's tacit ally, for what appeared in the record as rigorous and impatient stands on the part of the Commission, were in reality mostly posturing for public effect. Some of the member-governments were pressing the Commission to get Italy to reduce border taxes. They had to press the Commission in this manner because their own export industries were pressing on them. Therefore, to maintain its executive credibility the Commission had to appear to be going after Italy. On the other hand, the Commission was not interested in forcing the Italian Government into a domestic political crisis (and neither did the other EEC governments want this). The Community would have gained nothing from another Italian crisis, least of all the implementation of the Value Added Tax! Brussels therefore understood the dilemma facing Rome, and Rome understood that Brussels understood. 'The Commission understood Italian problems,' an Italian Finance Ministry official noted. 'But [they] could not be lenient since a number of countries had complied and the Commission was really in no position to accept non-compliance. They were morally sympathetic, but technically bound.'[45] The Commission and the Italian Government thus entered into a game of political charades where public pronouncements were moderated by private assurances. Most other member-governments were also aware of what was going on, and they tacitly approved, though they could not show this in public because, as noted, they were being pressed by their own export industries to get tough with Italy. The purpose of the game was to allow the Italian Government the time it needed to resolve its domestic political problems. This was in both Italy's and the Community's interest.

The Italian Government used the time thus gained to pacify the domestic resistance to the Value Added Tax, and thereby to create a political atmosphere that would support compliance with the EEC's VAT Directives. But since the Italian Government was fragile, pacification could not mean suppression. The Government could not simply ride roughshod over the opposition as ultimately happened in the Netherlands. Instead, the Italian Government had to find ways to accommodate all of the objections and demands for special consideration. In the end, therefore, the rates of the Italian VAT were adjusted to answer the concerns of the Left. Impositions on food and other necessities ranged from 1 to 3 percent instead of 6 to 12 percent as set for most other transactions. Export subsidies hidden in the old IGE were reportedly also built into the new VAT system to satisfy big business. Guarantees were offered to small businessmen to the effect that records maintained for VAT purposes would not be inspected for income tax purposes. Municipalities were similarly assured that the VAT would not wipe out local revenues, but that allocations from the central government would more than offset losses from withdrawn taxes. Meanwhile, analyses based on the proposed 6 and 12 percent rates convinced the Ministry of Finance that revenues from the VAT would be at least as great as those generated by the IGE. Public opinion was eventually lulled into accepting that substantial price increases would not necessarily follow upon the imposition of the VAT. Obviously, completing this elaborate pattern of political accommodation took time— about thirty-one months. But once the pattern was complete and all of the sidepayments were made, it again became politically safe for the Italian Government to join its EEC partners in moving toward European fiscal harmonization.

Italy and the VAT

In a broader perspective the Italian struggle with the Value Added Tax continued the pattern of political reverberation that had characterized the EEC policy process since the beginning of the fiscal harmonization movement. The adoption of the First and Second VAT Directives in the spring of 1967 brought to a close a period of intense political activity in Brussels which had lasted from December 1966 to April 1967. This culminated in the Franco-Dutch compromise that ended the Dutch impasse and opened the way to definitive action in the Council of Ministers. Prior to this the most consequential political activity surrounding EEC fiscal harmonization took place in the Dutch domestic arena. But then, as the present chapter has shown, the locus of politics shifted again and came to center in the Italian domestic arena. The political contest then shifted back to Brussels briefly in the autumn of 1969, then back to Italy until the spring of 1972, back to Brussels and finally back to Italy. When studied from a 'Brussels' perspective it appeared as if the fiscal harmonization process was moving in fits and starts, with short bursts of activity separated by long intervals of inaction. But, when the reverberations are taken into account it becomes clear that the politics of fiscal harmonization were in fact continuous. All of the action, however, did not take place in Brussels, and not very much of it was inter-governmental in nature. Most of it took place in Italy: it was *domestic* in nature, and, most significantly, it largely determined the substance, timing and tempo of that which took place in Brussels.

As in the Dutch case, but perhaps even more dramatically, the imperatives of European integration injected an issue into Italian politics that the Italians had no wish to deal with. Yet, they could not avoid the issue because their membership in the EEC obliged them to confront it. Once in the Italian public domain, the issue was immediately, widely and intensely politicized. It irritated almost universal sensitivities about bearing burdens of taxation in a country where such impositions are hardly appreciated. Furthermore, the European Communities in intruding into Italian fiscal affairs were essentially asking Italians to change their ways, to substitute an unfamiliar system for a familiar one and to exchange an eminently evadable system for one that theoretically had very few loopholes. All of this, moreover, hit the Italian polity suddenly in 1967 because public information policies had not prepared the way. Is it any wonder then that the VAT became a political football in Italy!

As in the West German and Dutch cases, Italian balking over the VAT had nothing at all to do with opposition to European integration or even to fiscal harmonization. Nor did it have to do with malevolence towards Brussels, or, as the journalists believed, with failed Italian political will. It was again a matter of *political incapacity*. Regardless of the fact that cooperation with EEC partners remained most desirable to Italian leaders, domestic pressures on the Government in Rome largely determined what was possible and impossible among policy choices. Under the circumstances it proved impossible to choose international cooperation for a long period of time. 'Italians accepted the logic and necessity of tax harmonization,' a Foreign Ministry official explained. 'Therefore it was never a question of wilful or deliberate attempts at obstruction. The problem was really with the implications of the VAT in Italy.'[46] Thus the Italian Government did not move on the VAT because it could not move. Resistance to the new tax was overwhelming, and failure to take heed would certainly have jeopardized the stability of the Government. By opposite token, when the Italian Government could move, it did. When the opposition to the VAT subsided, what earlier had been impossible among policy choices finally became possible. The Italian Government then moved rapidly into compliance with the VAT Directives and back into its preferred role as a staunch promoter of European unity.

The European Commission played a subtle, interesting and effective part in the Italian episode. Naturally the Commission's objective was to bring Italy into compliance as quickly as possible and to get the fiscal harmonization process and the Community's 'own resources' plan back on track. Yet the Commission was also aware that it could not force the Italian Government into compliance by activating legal mechanisms contained in the Rome Treaty. So-called 'Article 169 procedures' that lead stepwise from Commission policing to the European Court of Justice have rarely proven effective against member-states that choose to ignore them.[47] In addition, such procedures tend to be long and drawn-out and the Commission certainly saves no time in pursuing them. Here again it remains a fact that the EEC is an aggregation of sovereign states, and the authorities in Brussels ultimately cannot compel member-countries to act against their perceived interests.

Enforcement in the EEC setting then is much more often political rather than judicial. To pursue its objective of gaining Italian compliance with the VAT Directives the Commission had to enter into the politics set in motion by the Italian requests for postponement. Unlike in the Dutch case where the Commission acted almost like one of the member-governments and joined in efforts to 'flush' the resistance in The Hague, in the Italian episode the Commission acted more as a buffer and broker. As noted, the Commission was sensitive to the Italian domestic political situation, and it was aware that influential Italian journalists and other opinion-leaders were interpreting the international uproar over the proposed postponement of the VAT as an attempt on the part of other countries to neutralize Italy's competitiveness in trade. If in this situation the Commission had allied directly with those governments that were protesting most loudly about Italy's border taxes, VAT opponents within Italy, with their nationalism aroused, might have become even more obdurate. This would have made matters worse for the Rome Government and it would probably have prolonged the delay in implementing the VAT. Thus, the Commission chose instead to enter into the charade described earlier, where it absorbed the protests of the other member-governments and translated them into harsh-sounding admonishments directed at Rome. At the same time Italian officials were quietly assured that their political dilemmas were well understood in Brussels and that little biting was likely to accompany the Commission's loud barking. In constructing and pursuing this charade the Commission helped the Italian Government to find the time it needed to win over the domestic opposition to the VAT. This probably also helped to stave off a full-scale political crisis in Italy. Most importantly, it facilitated eventual Italian compliance and got European integration moving again in the fiscal field.

Notes

1. Materials presented in this chapter are drawn extensively from my previously published article, 'Domestic Politics and Regional Harmonization in the European Communities,' *World Politics*, Vol. 27, No. 4 (July 1975), pp. 467–95.
2. Andrew J. Taussig, 'The Impact of European Communities Upon German Ministries,' unpublished doctoral thesis, Harvard University, 1971, p. 188.
3. For a more comprehensive treatment of enforcement questions, see Puchala, 'Domestic Politics and Regional Harmonization . . . .', op. cit., *passim*.
4. *Agence Europe*, 5 May 1969; Interviews, Brussels, 16 March 1973.
5. *The Times*, London, 'Italian Fiscal Reform,' 22 June 1965; 'VAT to be Italy's First Step in Basic Reform of Taxation,' 19 October 1972.
6. *Agence Europe*, 16 October 1968; see also, Istituto per l'economia europea, *Le Implicazioni Politico Economicbe e Tecnico Amministrative Della Imposta Sul Valore Aggiunto in Italia*, Rome, 1968, pp. 137–69 *et passim*.
7. *Agence Europe*, 16 October 1968.

8. *Agence Europe*, 5 May 1969.
9. Ibid.; Article 101 makes provision for the Council to take action against member-states who distort competition on the Common Market by failing to bring domestic legislation into line with that of other states.
10. *Agence Europe*, 5 May 1969.
11. *Agence Europe*, 6 August 1969.
12. *Agence Europe*, 18 September 1969; 25 September 1969; 29 September 1969; 1 October 1969; 17–18 October 1969; 4 November 1969.
13. *Agence Europe*, 1 October 1969.
14. *Agence Europe*, 18 September 1969.
15. *Agence Europe*, 29 September 1969.
16. Ibid.
17. *Agence Europe*, 5 May 1969.
18. *Agence Europe*, 17–18 October 1969.
19. *Corriere Della Sera*, 'Tensione per l'IVA fra il MEC e l'Italia,' 14 October 1969.
20. Invoking Article 101 was in fact subject to national veto. See, *Treaty of Rome*, Art. 101, Para. 2.
21. Here the Commission would be proceeding under Article 169 of the Rome Treaty.
22. *Agence Europe*, 9 December 1969; Cf., also, *Third Council Directive of 9 December 1969 on the Harmonization of Legislation of Member States Concerning Turnover Taxes* COM (69) 862 final.
23. *Agence Europe*, 9 November 1970.
24. *Agence Europe*, 16 March 1972.
25. *Fifth Council Directive of 4 July 1972 on the Harmonization of Legislation of Member States Concerning Turnover Taxes*, COM(72) 344 final.
26. Interview, Rome, 26 March 1973.
27. See, for example, Norman Kogan, *The Government of Italy*, New York, Cromwell, 1962; Joseph G. LaPalombara, *Interest Groups in Italian Politics*, Princeton, N.J., Princeton University Press, 1964; Genevieve Bibes, *Le Système politique italien*, Paris, Presses universitaires de France, 1974.
28. Interview, Rome, 17 March 1973.
29. See, for example, *Corriere Della Sera*, 15 November 1969.
30. Interview, Rome, 13 March 1973.
31. See, for example, *Le Scelte Del Consumatore*, 'E presto l'IVA: quanto ci costera?' No. 1–2 (1972), pp. 34–6; *Le Scelte Del Consumatore*, 'I prezzi e l'IVA,' No. 9–10 (1972), p. 5.
32. See Chapter 3, p. 46.

33. Gianni Pasquarelli, 'Perche L'I.G.E. Sara Sostituta Dall l'IVA,' *Communita Europee*, No. 8/9 (1967), p. 13.
34. The continued Italian practice of 'little gifts' became particularly annoying to the other member-governments when their own introduction of the transparent VAT made such practices on their part more difficult.
35. Interviews, Rome, 13, 14 & 17 March 1973.
36. Interview, CGIL, Rome, 13 March 1973.
37. *Agence Europe*, 24 February 1975.
38. Raphael Zariski, *Italy: the Politics of Uneven Development*, Hindsdale, Ill., The Dryden Press, 1972, p. 120; See also *La Stampa*, Turin, 6 March 1970.
39. Interview, Rome, 13 March 1973.
40. *Corriere Della Sera*, 2 October 1969; 15 November 1969.
41. *Corriere Della Sera*, 15 November 1969. Studies reported here estimated between 35 percent and 50 percent evasion under the IGE.
42. *The Times*, London, 9 August 1971.
43. Interview, Rome, 13 March 1973.
44. *Agence Europe*, 7 December 1971; 15 December 1971; 21 April 1972.
45. Interview, Rome, 13 March 1973.
46. Interview, Rome, 17 March 1973; cf., also, Donald J. Puchala and Carl Lankowski, 'The Politics of Fiscal Harmonization in the European Communities,' *Journal of Common Market Studies*, Vol. 15, No. 3 (March 1977), pp. 155–79.
47. Puchala, 'Domestic Politics and Regional Harmonization . . .,' op. cit., pp. 512–13.

6

Britain confronts the Community

British experience with the EEC's Value Added Tax occurred in two phases. The first lasted from 1970 to 1973. By the time the United Kingdom initiated its third bid for entry into the Common Market in June 1970, the First and Second Community VAT Directives had already been adopted and the VAT was being collected in most of the member-states. It was assumed that the United Kingdom would introduce the tax if and when it entered Europe. Accordingly, the British Government introduced a Value Added Tax in April 1973, exactly three months after the UK joined the Common Market.

However, it is not entirely accurate to conclude that Britain introduced the VAT because it was obliged to do so by the European Community. The VAT was also the cornerstone of a program of fiscal reform conceived by the Conservative Party and pursued with some vigor after its electoral victory in June 1970. Many Tory supporters of the tax reform wanted the VAT regardless of the Common Market bid or its result. But, because the political contests in Britain over Common Market membership and domestic fiscal reform occurred at nearly the same time, and because the VAT was an issue in both contests, the politics of VAT were complicated and obfuscated by the politics of Europe.

The second phase in Britain's involvement with the Community Value Added Tax lasted from 1973 to 1976. Even before the First and Second VAT Directives were fully in force, the European Commission began work on what was to become the Sixth VAT Directive.[1] This was to be the next move forward toward the abolition of fiscal frontiers wherein the member-governments would agree upon a common list of goods and services that would be subject to the VAT.

Creating such a 'common base' was both the next logical harmonizing step and also a crucially important prerequisite to the Community's 'own resources' scheme. It was also an integral element of movement toward Economic and Monetary Union. Thus, no sooner were the British in the EEC and dutifully collecting the VAT than they were asked by Brussels to begin modifying the tax to make it look more European. For reasons of domestic politics in Great Britain, where European symbols were not terribly popular, and where, after February 1974, a Labour Government was attempting to renegotiate the terms of British membership, London would not consider modifying the British VAT. One of the main issues surrounding the Sixth Directive therefore became the question of whether the British VAT was to become more like the one that Brussels wanted, or whether Brussels could be persuaded to want something that was more like what the British already had.

The two phases of the British VAT experience were linked in a manner that is most revealing in terms of this book's themes. Domestic politics in the UK during the earlier phase constrained British diplomatic flexibility during the later phase. Negotiations toward the Sixth Directive after 1973 proved most sensitive for the British Government because of political commitments made domestically before 1973. In order to assure support for the legislation that created the British VAT, the Government had to incorporate into it many of the sacred cows of British fiscal tradition, including a rather wide range of exemptions and so-called *zero ratings* that allowed certain transactions to go untaxed. These practices were permitted as transitional measures under the Community's Second VAT Directive, but they were to be nullified by the Sixth.[2] Since it was believed that European fiscal harmonization could not proceed toward a common base for the VAT as long as the British were exempting goods and services that others were taxing, London's practices were challenged by other member-governments and the Commission. However, if the British Government yielded to Community pressures, it would thereby have reneged on past commitments to domestic constituents and opened a political Pandora's box at home. Yet, if it did not yield, and indeed it did not have to because of the Council's unanimity rules, the common base for the VAT could not be established, and everything in Community planning that depended upon this would be imperiled. This set the scene for a classic political contest.

The British VAT

Many of those involved in the planning and promoting that produced the British Value Added Tax in April 1973 argue vehemently to this day that the introduction of the new tax had almost nothing to do with the fact that the United Kingdom was joining the Common Market. The tax was needed, they say, and it would have been introduced in the UK even if negotiations for entry into the EEC had never opened. Yet there are at the same time any number of others in Great Britain, who were also involved in the events that led to the VAT, who argue equally forcefully that the British VAT had absolutely everything to do with the EEC and the enlargement negotiations. Had Britain not joined the Common Market, these spokesmen contend, there never would have been a British VAT.

These alternative interpretations oversimplify the motives of VAT proponents and detractors in the debates over British fiscal reform. Some of those who supported the Heath Government's proposed reform of indirect taxation during 1971 and 1972 did so for European reasons pure and simple: accepting the tax was part of paying the price of admission into the Common Market. Others favored the tax because they believed it to be an appropriate response to some real fiscal problems. Still others joined the pro-VAT coalition for reasons of party loyalty, or from fear of political reprisals from the party leadership, or because they had been favored with sidepayments from the Tory Government. Similarly, among opponents to the VAT, some rejected the tax because it was a European symbol—a 'nasty foreign tax.' Others saw it as a regressive, inflationary 'Tory tax' and condemned it as a fiscal device. Still others joined the opposition out of party loyalty. What is most remarkable, although probably not extraordinary in political contests such as this, is that the great majority of those involved in either promoting or opposing the British VAT thoroughly misperceived one another's motives. This was particularly true with regard to the extent to which contenders believed each other to be influenced by European or anti-European sympathies. So too did many involved misperceive the degree to which Brussels authorities intervened in the British debates. In fact they intervened very little, but many VAT opponents believed that the EEC was almost dictating to the Heath Government.

Ultimately there is no definite answer to whether there would have been a British VAT if the UK had not joined the Common Market. The strength of the Conservative leadership's commitment to fiscal reform after the 1970 election and its choice of the Value Added Tax as the primary vehicle suggest that the tax probably would have been introduced regardless of the European outcome.[3] But this begs the question of why the VAT was chosen to be the vehicle of the Tory-sponsored tax reform, and leaves undetermined the extent to which European aspirations might have conditioned the choice.[4] On these and other questions concerning the politics of British fiscal reform there is no way to untangle the reformers' domestic concerns and the marketeers' desires to demonstrate good Europeanism. As in the other VAT cases already examined, European issues during this British episode complicated domestic ones, and these then reverberated to cause problems in Brussels. Exactly how this happened makes a revealing story. Furthermore, understanding what happened in Britain with regard to the VAT before 1973 is absolutely essential to understanding what later happened in Brussels.

British Fiscal Reform

In partial support of those who contend that the British Value Added Tax evolved from a fiscal analysis that had little to do with British aspirations for EEC membership, it is true that from the late 1950s onward fiscal reform was an important, independent issue on the agendas of British governments. Economically and financially speaking, the need for reform followed from two sets of problems. First, many analysts felt that the comparatively lower rates of economic growth that the United Kingdom was experiencing in the 1960s, particularly *vis-à-vis* its neighbors on the Continent, were due in some measure to the heavy emphasis on direct taxation in the British system.[5] High personal income taxes affected savings, and corporation taxes affected costs that raised export prices. On the Continent by contrast, direct taxes played a lesser role in fiscal affairs, thereby lowering corporate costs. Moreover, indirect taxes were rebated at national frontiers, thus neutralizing their impacts on export prices. Britishers therefore felt a need to do something to their fiscal system that would stimulate their economy and contribute to making their exports more competitive.

There were also growing concerns in the UK about finding sources of government revenue. As in most countries in the post-war era, public expenditures in the United Kingdom were rising rapidly and revenue collections strained to keep pace. Up to the mid 1960s the Government increased its revenues by raising income and profits taxes, by increasing excises on items such as alcohol, tobacco and petrol, and by raising the rates of its Purchase Tax. This latter was a sales tax levied at the wholesale stage on a range of consumer goods that 'were neither essentials nor regarded as necessary for the normal daily needs of the average British household.'[6] The Purchase Tax exempted food, children's clothing, utilities, transportation and a great many other mass consumption goods and services. But the problem with this and most of the other taxes was that their rates were approaching levels at which disincentives to consumption were beginning to generate diminishing returns in revenue.[7] Harold Wilson's Labour Government in 1966 added a Selective Employment Tax (SET) to the British array of fiscal instruments and thereby boosted public revenue by imposing upon certain white-collar and service industry payrolls.[8] This eased the revenue problem.

But for the Conservative Party the fiscal system was also creating political problems. Its progressive structure and increasing levies were hitting hardest at classes and sectors that accounted for the greatest number of Tory voters. Pressures for tax relief were therefore mounting among party supporters. As one British respondent with decided Conservative leanings explained: the high income taxes were 'abusive to well-to-do people' who were after all 'Tory clients,' while the Purchase Tax had 'discriminatory rates against all things a reasonably successful person would want to buy.'[9] As for the SET, the Conservatives saw this as imposing further penalties on their supporters in the white-collar ranks. In addition, they accused the Labour Party of breaking an election promise by instituting the tax, and they pledged in no uncertain terms to abolish it as soon as a Tory Government returned to office.[10]

Introducing a Value Added Tax was one way to broaden the base of indirect taxation and to guarantee an increased flow of revenue. It also opened a way to shifting from heavy reliance on income taxes. The VAT idea was considered briefly in Britain in 1963 and 1964, at the time that the European Communities were also studying the new tax. But a Committee on Turnover Taxation appointed by the Conservative Government then in office found 'no valid reason, on a comparison of the two systems, for the introduction of a value-added tax in place of the purchase tax.'[11] The Committee reported that the tax would not appreciably help exports and that the costs of establishing and administering it would be immense. The Conservative Party therefore initially rejected the VAT idea. Labour was somewhat more positive, and Harold Wilson appeared taken for a time with the notion of a VAT for the United Kingdom.[12] But by the time of the second British bid for entry into the Common Market in 1967 Labour's attitude toward the VAT had cooled appreciably, partly because of the potential inflationary impacts of the tax, and also because of the complexities of implementation. While Wilson was leading the drive for entry into the EEC, Labour unenthusiastically accepted the tax as a price that would have to be paid for admission into Europe. But the party quickly dismissed the VAT when the entry bid failed.

But in the meantime the idea of a British VAT had again come up for serious consideration within the Conservative Party. While in opposition between 1964 and 1970 the Party initiated a program of research and planning in preparation for an eventual return to office. The work was carried on at the Party's Central Office by study groups composed of Members of Parliament, often of Shadow Cabinet status, senior party officials and academics and other consultants.[13] The Economic Policy Group which considered fiscal matters was chaired by Edward Heath. In going once again through the exigencies of fiscal reform, both economic and political —i.e., income tax relief, export competitiveness, revenue requirements and the hard and fast Tory commitment to abolish the SET—the Economic Policy Group arrived at the need for a new broad-based sales tax.[14] Expanding the base of the Purchase Tax was rejected, partly for technical reasons involving exemptions, but mainly because introducing a Value Added Tax was most compatible with the Conservative leadership's ambition to ultimately join the European Community. At this point European concerns and matters of domestic fiscal reform became entangled, and the European hopes of the Tory leaders, Edward Heath in particular, restricted the range of conceivable turnover tax options to one. 'Part of Conservative policy,' a former member of the Economic Policy Group recalled,

was the determination to go into Europe, and the compelling reason for the VAT was that it coincided with European policy. In this sense it really had to be VAT and no other kind of indirect tax.[15]

Iain Macleod included the proposed VAT as a formal part of Conservative policy at the Party's Annual Conference at Brighton in October 1969.[16]

The Struggle in Parliament

Had the Labour Party won the general election of June 1970, and had the third bid for Common Market membership still proved successful, the Wilson leadership would have accepted the VAT as the price of admission into Europe. There would have been little Conservative opposition on this point, and the reform of British turnover taxes would have been a relatively uncontroversial, though not terribly popular, *fait accompli*. But the Tories won in 1970, and this entirely changed the political context within which the tax reform and the VAT proposal were debated. For one thing, as Labour shifted in 1971 into opposing Common Market membership 'on Tory terms,' party spokesmen became less and less constrained in attacking the proposed British VAT. They had little use for it except as a European entry ticket, and when entry was no longer desirable for them they readily tore up the ticket. In addition, while the leadership of the Conservative Party naturally wanted both Common Market membership and fiscal reform, the backbenches and the constituencies were not uniformly supportive on the two matters. There were some who favored Europe but who had misgivings about the VAT, while there were others who recognized the merit in domestic fiscal reform but none the less joined the anti-marketeers on Europe. Complicating the situation further, there were some, as noted earlier, who supported the VAT *because* they wanted Britain in Europe, and some who rejected the VAT precisely *because* it symbolized Europe. Conservative leaders therefore encountered problems of presentation: should they link the two issues and capitalize upon Europeanism, or should they separate them to minimize the effects of anti-Europeanism? Given the unpopularity of European matters in public opinion in the early 1970s, and the uncertain strength of the Europeans in Parliament, the Conservative leadership leaned toward insulating the VAT discussions. Mr Barber and Mr Higgins therefore pushed fiscal reform on its merits and deliberately tried to separate the issue from the European debates.[17]

The Heath Government's commitment to introduce a Value Added Tax was made formally in the spring of 1971 and contained in a Green Paper presented to Parliament by the Chancellor of the Exchequer.[18] Without going into great detail, the Green Paper notified Parliament that a tax reform was in the offing and that two major elements were to be the introduction of a VAT and the abolition of the SET.[19] A bill presenting the Value Added Tax in detail was promised for the autumn of 1971. But drafting was delayed until March 1972 when a White Paper on the VAT was attached as part of the Chancellor's budget proposals for 1973.[20]

In his Budget Speech on 22 March 1972 Anthony Barber called for a Value Added Tax at a standard rate of 10 percent.

It would replace both the Selective Employment Tax and the Purchase Tax. Certain services such as education, health, insurance and the post would be exempted from the VAT as would new housing and rents. Most food items would be zero-rated and so would newspapers, books and periodicals. Furthermore, the tax would not be imposed in the agricultural sector or on small businesses whose annual turnover was less than £5,000 (or approximately $14,000). The new tax would take effect on 1 April 1973.[21]

Almost everything about the proposed VAT turned out to be politically controversial; the contests over the tax centered in the House of Commons and stretched over two years, from the spring of 1971 to the spring of 1973. There were at least two separate but parallel campaigns in the political fray. One divided the front and back benches of the Conservative Party; the other pitted the two parties, Conservative against Labour. Recurrent confrontations over the VAT surrounded successive Government moves along the pathway from proposal to bill, to law, to enforcement. But since the alignments and debates were similar from instance to instance, it is less important to examine the length and breadth of the contest than it is to look into the motives and tactics of the contenders. It is also especially important in terms of this book's purpose to examine and to assess the ways in which European themes were woven into the VAT debates.

The experience of the Economic Policy Group during the mid-1960s had united most of the leaders of the Conservative Party in favor of fiscal reform and the VAT. However, the parliamentary party was far from united on these issues, largely because Tory supporters in the constituencies had problems with the VAT. The proposed tax was poorly understood, and, as noted, it was generally unpopular among British voters. Since it was to reach the retail stage and cover a long list of goods and services that had not been theretofore taxed in the United Kingdom, it appeared to be an immense departure from previous fiscal practice, and many saw it leading to across-the-board price increases.[22] Among traditional Tory supporters, the owners of small and medium-sized businesses were particularly upset with the proposed

VAT for all of the 'bookkeeping' reasons that bothered their counterparts in other EEC countries. 'Small business people hated the bloody thing,' one MP recalled.[23] Local chambers of commerce and various trade associations for small business made their displeasure known to the Tory MPs who represented them, as did groups standing for the interests of housewives and mothers who anticipated new taxes on everyday family goods.[24] Many Tory backbenchers were thus subjected to uncomfortable political cross-pressures: parliamentary Whips, who influenced MPs' future careers, wanted unwavering support for the tax reform as proposed by the leadership, while local committees, which influenced nominations and elections, wanted all manner of concessions for their special interests.[25]

Within the parliamentary Conservative Party then, backbenchers pressed the leadership to amend the VAT Bill in ways that would make the new tax more acceptable in the constituencies. The main issue was exemptions. Various backbenchers sought tax-free status or zero-ratings for extensive lists of items that were sensitive in their constituencies. 'Everyone wanted to be exempted from the VAT,' a Conservative MP explained, 'and local committees told us about this.'[26] Mr Barber and his colleagues, however, wanted as few exemptions as possible in the VAT system, partly because each one narrowed the base of the tax and thus either reduced revenue or required higher rates on remaining taxable transactions. In addition, Conservative leaders feared a snowballing of demands for exemptions and thus hesitated to grant any but the ones that were included in the Chancellor's 1972 budget message. These alone exempted more than 30 percent of the British economy!

To impress the leadership with the seriousness of their concerns the backbenchers lobbied in the House of Commons and organized letter-writing and signature-gathering campaigns in their constituencies. In one instance, for example, some Tory backbenchers working with the London *Daily Mail* gathered more than one million signatures to support amendments to the VAT Bill which would exempt children's shoes and clothing. Moreover, on at least three occasions during the parliamentary proceedings on the VAT Bill, backbench Tories threatened to break party discipline and to either abstain or join the opposition in protest over the leadership's refusal to accept amendments.[27] For their part the leadership whipped the parliamentary party with appeals for unity, with promises to certain MPs about their political futures, and with threats about similar matters to particularly rebellious members. Some concessions were ultimately offered which exempted children's shoes and clothing and certain medicines from the VAT. But in the end party discipline was effectively enforced and most backbench requests for preferential treatment were rejected.[28]

European or anti-European leanings did not play a significant part in the Conservatives' intra-party struggle over the VAT. There were rumblings among Tory anti-marketeers about Mr Heath's zeal in promoting the VAT as 'a gesture of European good faith.'[29] Some suspected, and suggested, that the gesture was mainly intended to influence the entry negotiations going on in Brussels and that the party leadership cared much more about these than about tax reform in the United Kingdom. There were also suspicions that the party leaders' resistance to amendments and concessions in the VAT Bill followed from the fact that for European reasons they wanted the British VAT to look as nearly like the EEC VAT as possible. Or, some supposed that Mr Heath and his colleagues were under direct pressure from Brussels and that the form and content of the new tax were being prescribed by the Eurocracy.[30] Nevertheless, the Conservative Party did not divide along European/anti-European lines in its infighting over the VAT, and in the voting in the House of Commons it hardly divided at all. Yet, in more subtle ways, the results of the intra-party struggle, and particularly the certain exemptions that the Tory leadership finally granted, were to have later repercussions in the course of European fiscal harmonization. These, however, are best assessed after the inter-party contest has been examined.

The Labour Party's attack on the Conservatives' proposed VAT was never meant to be an effort to defeat either the VAT idea or the Government's Bill. Even with some defections in the back benches, the Tory majority was large enough to assure passage of whatever the parliamentary leadership chose to press. Therefore, Labour sought not to block the tax reform *per se*, but rather to ultimately unseat the Tories by ridiculing the VAT before the British electorate. Naturally, the VAT was not the only Conservative initiative that Labour was criticizing in public for electoral reasons, but it was one on which political capital could be accumulated because the tax was unpopular and the Tories were therefore politically exposed on the issue. Labour hammered relentlessly on four themes: (1) that the tax would be regressive and inflationary, (2) that administering the VAT system would be a costly nightmare for all concerned, (3) that the tax represented a humiliating kowtowing to the European Communities, and (4) that the tax was but a first step in a pattern of fiscal integration in the Common Market that would lead eventually to the loss of national budgetary autonomy and the abolition of practices sacred to British fiscal tradition.

Because the Labour criticism was intended to embarrass rather than persuade the Conservatives and since it was designed more for media consumption than parliamentary debate, the attack was both colorful and vituperative. For example:

—In April 1971, Harold Wilson attacked the proposed VAT as a fiscal 'monstrosity' and underlined that,

> if Mr Heath wants to introduce this masochistic gesture as a means of buying his way into Europe, this is something for us to evaluate when we know the terms on which Britain would enter . . . But if this is put forward . . . as a tax reform in its own right, then we fight it for what it is, regressive, reactionary, a tax not on business, or on goods you are free to buy, but a tax on necessities.[31]

— During the budget debates in May 1972, Shadow Cabinet Chancellor Dennis Healey described the proposed VAT as 'infinitely less economic than the taxes it replaced, open to evasion on a colossal scale, teeming with anomalies and likely to be highly inflationary in effect.'[32]

— In the same speech, Mr Healey went on to point out that,

> the Government thought they could get it on the statute book with a minimum of political fuss. It was [their] firm intention to change the yield, the coverage and the rate in coming years. They intended

to do so under the cover and under the protection of the argument that [they were] obliged to harmonize the rates and coverage with other European countries.[33]

—Labour MP Peter Shore, in a letter to *The Times* in March 1973, echoed the 'loss of sovereignty' theme by reminding readers that the VAT,

is the first measure in the history of Britain which no future British Parliament has the power to repeal as long as the Treaty of Accession remains in force [and] it is again the first tax in our history a substantial part of which . . . is permanently alienated to the Community's institutions.[34]

—Reflecting Labour's criticism of the complexity of the VAT's administrative workings, and adding some characteristic British sarcasm, another *Times* correspondent called the tax 'Gilbertian' and related that under the new fiscal regime,

a 'taxable person' bears no tax unless he becomes in any way exempt. The more exempt he becomes, the more tax he bears until, if he is wholly exempt he bears the whole tax he pays. Finally if you are not 'a taxable person' you both pay and bear the VAT in full.[35]

Upon recollection, most Labour Party supporters confirm that the party reaped political gains as a result of the assault on the VAT, and most Conservatives agree that this was probably the case.[36] Most also agree that the tax reform issue became as highly politicized and exploitable as it did because it was also a European issue. VAT opponents used the tax issue to fire anti-Europeanism and vice versa. All of this was to sow seeds for the next general election and for 'consulting the people' on the question of remaining in the Common Market.[37] The public was generally averse to Common Market membership between 1971 and 1973 and easily aroused by anti-European symbols and slogans. In addition, there were also sizeable numbers of anti-marketeers among nominal Tory supporters, and Labour hoped to woo them over by embarrassing Mr Heath and his colleagues about 'foreign' things like the Value Added Tax.[38] The VAT was an issue, albeit not a central one, in the general elections of February and October 1974, and Labour's earlier assault on the tax, on anti-European and other grounds, unquestionably helped the Party at the polls. Railing against the VAT continued to be good politics for Labour anti-marketeers right up to the time of the Referendum.[39]

There were also longer-term implications of the Labour assault on the VAT that were to become important in British dealings with other EEC members on questions of fiscal harmonization between 1973 and 1976. During the VAT debates in the House of Commons, the Conservatives were particularly sensitive to Labour's allegations that the coverage of the new tax and its rates would eventually have to be adjusted to meet EEC obligations. Labour spokesmen in the House of Commons, and their extra-parliamentary allies and clients, like the Trades Union Congress, drummed away with the accusation that the Tories planned sooner or later to impose the VAT on food and other necessities that had always been tax free in the United Kingdom.[40] The British people felt very strongly about the special tax status for necessities and trusted the British Government to steadfastly protect this aspect of fiscal tradition. But the Labour critics maintained that the zero-ratings on everyday goods could not continue indefinitely because Brussels would not permit this. Moreover, Labour insisted that the Tories were well aware of this and were therefore in the process of knowingly selling out British tradition. But, the more emphatic that Labour became in insisting that the Tories were deceiving the British people in order to please the 'foreigners' in Brussels, the more resolute the Conservatives became in affirming that they would never impose a sales tax on food and on the other traditionally exempted items that were untaxed or zero-rated in the British VAT system.

In light of the earlier discussion of tensions between Tory backbenchers and the party leadership, it now also becomes clear that the highly visible Conservative commitments to defend the exemptions and zero-ratings against EEC challenges were not only rebuttals to Labour and reassurances to the general public, but also pledges to the party's own backbenches and constituencies. Moreover, because of back-bench successes in gaining concessions on a number of items that the Conservative leadership initially wanted to tax, the Government's commitment to defend 'socially desirable' exemptions turned out to be broader than perhaps the party leadership would have liked. None the less, by the time that the VAT Bill was finalized and passed in July 1972, the Conservative Government was politically, and ever so firmly, locked into keeping everyday necessities free from the turn-over tax. Naturally, by their allegations against the Tories, the Labour party supporters also firmly committed themselves to preserving these exemptions, so that not only the present Government but also possible future ones were equally well locked in. Hence, as a British civil servant pointedly phrased it, there was to be 'no fiddling with food.'[41]

The Sixth VAT Directive

Less than one month after the British Government introduced its Value Added Tax, EEC Commissioner Henri Simonet informed Mr Heath and his colleagues that the zero-ratings and other exemptions on everyday goods would have to be abolished. With characteristic understatement *The Times* of London opined that this was 'likely to lead to a politically embarrassing row.'[42] The 'row' lasted two years.

As noted earlier, the collision course that was to run the British Government headlong into the Brussels authorities in the fiscal area was fixed even before the United Kingdom joined the Common Market. Ideas for the Sixth Directive, concerning a common base for the VAT, were under discussion in EEC working groups as early as 1967. Drafts were circulating in 1968. But because of the Italian postponements the Commission withheld formal proposal until June 1973.[43] All the while, the British Government was fully aware that the Community was moving toward the Sixth Directive and that this might require all member-states to apply the VAT to a common and comprehensive list of items that would include food and most of the other 'necessities' that were exempted or zero-rated in the British system. This incidentally lent some credibility to the VAT critics' allegations that the Conservatives intended to sell out to the EEC on the VAT as soon as they joined. British officials were also aware of the importance of a harmonized

VAT base as a prerequisite to the EEC's 'own resources' scheme scheduled for 1975, and of its importance as a step toward the abolition of fiscal frontiers which was crucial to the completion of Economic and Monetary Union. This too puzzled VAT critics as well as British Europeans (and anti-Europeans) who wondered how the Government could claim to be committed to Europe and to fiscal harmonization, but also to a VAT system that was quite different from the one that Brussels preferred.[44] In the thinking of the British Government, however, the apparent contradiction was easily resolved: the European Community would have to amend their VAT to look more like the British one!

London's inflexible stand against standardizing the VAT on Continental terms was naturally the result of the domestic politics that surrounded the establishment of the British VAT. In light of the political pledges that both parties had made to defend the numerous exemptions in their turnover tax, neither the Heath Government nor the Wilson Government that succeeded it was politically able to make the kind of adjustments in the British VAT that the Community was seeking. Indeed, neither the Conservative nor the Labour Government was even willing to consider this.[45] When asked during an interview about the UK's response during negotiations on the Sixth Directive to EEC pressures for British conformity, a Conservative official said that 'we told them to take a running jump.'[46] A Labour counterpart indicated that 'we simply ignored them. That was the only thing to do.'[47] Labour fortified its commitment to defend the VAT exemptions by pledging to secure EEC approval for them when it renegotiated the terms of British accession.[48]

But the EEC was also politically locked in. The Commission had a strong interest in seeing to it that the 'own resources' mechanism was set into motion quickly, and that the 1 percent of the VAT earmarked for Brussels amounted to as large a sum as possible. British footdragging was annoying because the 1975 deadline for the new Community financing scheme was rapidly approaching, and budgetary pressures were mounting in Brussels.[49] Permitting the British to operate their VAT system at variance with those of most other member-states was inequitable because with their narrower tax base the British would be paying less into the Community treasury. But adjusting the Community VAT to accommodate the British was also unacceptable because this would narrow the VAT base all over the Community and markedly reduce total revenues. Relatedly, the Commission was also concerned about the ultimate abolition of fiscal frontiers and about Economic and Monetary Union. Here their frustration was not so much over the way in which the VAT base was to be harmonized, but over the fact that the political deadlock with the British was keeping it from being harmonized at all. The longer the deadlock, the more elusive became the fiscal component of the EMU.

The Commission was forcefully backed by the Governments of West Germany and France.[50] German objections to either permitting the British VAT to operate as a special case, or to modifying the EEC system to suit the British were wholly practical. The German Government sought to make as modest a budgetary contribution to the EEC as possible, and it did not care to see its assessment raised because the British share was lowered. Nor did it care to see the British gaining competitive advantages because a range of their business transactions was subsidized by virtue of being zero-rated under the VAT.[51] French authorities seconded both of the West German points. They were also somewhat fearful that by allowing VAT exemptions anywhere in the Community, they would expose themselves to domestic interest groups who would demand similar treatment.

The French Government also had some deeper and more philosophical concerns. As during the Dutch episode, the French were again displeased with the untidyness of the British VAT system. The zero-ratings allowed for deductions backward that were not offset by shifting any tax forward. This, the French believed, 'upset the whole logic of the VAT and destroyed its elegance.'[52] But at an even more fundamental level the French questioned the philosophical roots of the British fiscal tradition. For the French, and others on the Continent, the fiscal system in theory was primarily a revenue-raising mechanism of the state. Taxes were intended to bring in the greatest possible amount of revenue while they registered the lowest possible distorting impacts on business and the national economy. By contrast, in British fiscal theory taxes are considered to be social and economic as well as revenue-raising instruments. They have been traditionally used to redistribute wealth, to encourage and discourage varieties of investments, and to prime and prune economic forces. French authorities interpreted the British inflexibility on the Sixth Directive to be a stand against Continental fiscal theory, and an attempt to infuse British theory and practice into the EEC. They wanted none of this.[53]

In the course of long and sometimes heated debates, compromises on the Sixth Directive were reached in steps during 1974 and 1975. They were mostly concessions to London. First, the Commission yielded to the British position and relaxed its opposition to exemptions and zero-ratings.[54] These would be permitted, the Commission allowed, as long as national contributions to the Community budget *included sums that would have been collected if the VAT had been levied on a common base that included the various nationally exempted and zero-rated items*. In this way the list of taxable goods and services would in fact be standardized Community-wide, and member-governments would be assessed 1 percent of the total turnover of the list. But items that would actually be taxed nationally would be decided by national governments. The Community VAT then would be commonly based but differentially applied in the member-states. If some governments chose not to apply the tax to some items on the Community's list, the shortfalls in VAT receipts owed to Brussels would be made up out of national treasuries.

In making this concession the Commission never abandoned its intention to eventually standardize the application of the VAT and to abolish nationally peculiar exemptions. But two considerations pertinent in the summer of 1973 prompted M. Simonet and his colleagues to relax their position *vis-à-vis* the British Government. On the one hand, the time was approaching where the mechanism for the 'own resources' system would have to be put in place, or the whole venture was going to have to be postponed, perhaps even scrapped. If the 1-percent-of-VAT component could not be confirmed by 1974, 'own resources' surely could not begin by 1975. It had become abundantly clear to the Commissioners during 1973 that British interests had to be accommodated or there would be no agreement by 1974. Relatedly, while the urgent timetable for 'own resources' heightened the need for agreement of some kind concerning the VAT, the lagging timetable for Economic and Monetary Union made it less imperative that the agreement include a common base, commonly applied. After the international monetary disruptions of 1971, the shift to floating exchange rates and the tribulations of the 'snakes' and 'tunnels,' it was gradually accepted in Brussels that EMU was receding into the distance. This lessened the urgency of having a commonly-applied VAT that would lead readily to a harmonization of rates and then directly to the abolition of fiscal frontiers. This would come about at some future time, the Commission still hoped, but much later than the initial EMU timetable anticipated. The EMU had thus become a future aspiration instead of a near-term plan, and under these circumstances the Commission felt it could live with the second-best solution of a commonly-based but differentially-applied VAT.

Other member-governments, however, were apparently less willing to distort the Community VAT to suit British interests. There was among member-governments a general understanding of the domestic political causes of London's inflexibility.[55] The Irish Government was in the same position as the British, and to some extent the Danes and Italians felt similarly pressed regarding VAT exemptions and could therefore empathize with London. Neither did the West Germans or the French have any desire to prompt a crisis in the UK, particularly since the whole question of continuing British membership was intensely at issue there in 1974. But the Continental governments wanted a genuine compromise that would reflect their interests as well as the UK's. In the end the compromise employed a rather standard EEC formula: agreement was reached by pushing the controversial issues into the future.

In the intricate wording of Article 28 of the Sixth VAT Directive, national peculiarities in the VAT that had been permitted in Article 17 of the Second Directive were abolished —*but not immediately*. Instead, such things as exemptions and zero-ratings were again accepted as 'transitional measures' that could be practiced 'until such a date as shall be fixed by the Council on a proposal from the Commission.'[56] By this wording the French Government (and the Commission) could feel that they had gained British agreement to eventually abolish their system of exemptions and zero-ratings. They also believed that they had procured British acceptance of the principle of a revenue-earning, socially and economically neutral turnover tax, a key element of the Continental fiscal philosophy. The Germans and others who were more interested in the competition-distorting effects of British tax exemptions saw in Article 28 a means of keeping London under pressure to suspend their deviant practices because the Commission was instructed to monitor and report on national behavior during the transitional period. For their part, the British saw in Article 28 a grant of unlimited continuance for their exemptions and zero-ratings. These could be removed only by agreement in the Council of Ministers where the UK held a veto. The Sixth Directive then merely postponed further debate on unsettled questions. But in the short run, the British got just about everything they wanted.

Though it was probably the most important, the controversy over exemptions and zero-ratings was only one of the many disputes surrounding the Sixth Directive. Debates over countless technical points continued through 1975 and 1976, and the negotiations became so tedious that the European Parliament was prompted to register its impatience by reporting 'the impression that the lengthy procedure in the Council is due to the absence of political will.'[57] Largely because of the delays over the Sixth Directive, the 'own resources' plan had to be twice postponed and did not take effect until 1979. Agreement on the text of the Sixth Directive was finally achieved in the Council of Ministers in March 1977 and the Sixth Directive was adopted in May. Ironically, the United Kingdom chaired these final meetings.

British Politics and the Community VAT

The British experience with the Value Added Tax exhibited some interesting variations on themes recurrent in this book. In the British case, as in the German and Italian, European issues and imperatives complicated the politics surrounding national tax reform. But unlike the other cases, the European symbolism that attached to the Value Added Tax in the United Kingdom hindered the advocates of tax reform as much as it helped them. European symbols tended to politicize the VAT issue more than might otherwise have been the case, and in the UK they were at least as effective in mobilizing opposition as in rallying support for the new tax or for the Conservative Government that was promoting it. To do something because it was the European thing to do was not entirely politic in the British context between 1971 and 1973. The Tories were therefore forced to waffle on the European implications of the VAT. For their part, Labour had a field day with the issue of the 'nasty foreign tax' and this ultimately proved politically helpful to them and costly to the Conservatives.

Again the contrast between this British situation and those earlier observed in other EEC countries must be underlined. In Germany, Italy and the Netherlands governments could push through controversial legislation in politically sensitive areas by associating their actions with European goals or imperatives. Clearly, this was not true in the UK. These differences in the domestic effects of European symbolism followed in considerable measure from contrasting British and Continental experiences in the post-war era and from generally varying historical traditions. Psychologically, some Britishers were Europeans, but most were not and did not want to be, and this explains a good deal about their reactions to European symbols. But, in addition, the political atmosphere of European Community affairs was not the same in the 1970s, when the British confronted the Sixth Directive, as it had been a decade earlier, when the original Six hammered out the First and Second Directives. Europe was losing its domestic political appeal, not only in Britain, but in other EC countries as well. National concessions in the interest of European unity were coming to be less well-received among electorates than had earlier been the case, and 'good European' reputations were becoming liabilities in some national contexts. In this sense, the politically questionable implications of Europeanism in domestic affairs manifested in the UK during the VAT episode were early reflections of patterns that were to become more common throughout the Community in the later 1970s and early 1980s. It was no longer sufficient to explain to elites and electorates that something was or had to be done in the interest of Europe. To be politically acceptable domestically the strict and narrow national interest had to be served as well.

The conceptual distinction between *political capacity* and *political will* also adds to the understanding of the British VAT experience, but again in a way that is somewhat different from the other cases. With regard to the West German, Dutch and Italian episodes it was concluded that delays, obstructionist behavior and other national interference with the flow and tempo of the EC policy process were caused by domestic political incapacities and not by failures of political will. The national governments in question *wanted* to comply with the Commission's proposals and Community directives, but for reasons of domestic politics they temporarily could not. Intermittent 'bad Europeanism,' however, in no way diluted firm and continuing commitments to European integration.

In the British episode this was not so obviously the case. During the negotiations concerning the Sixth Directive the British Government unquestionably lacked the political capacity to accommodate Continental preferences. Tories and Labour alike were constrained by their previous commitments and any wavering would have been costly to both intra-party unity and electoral credibility. But, at the same time the British Government never really exhibited any desire to comply with Community preferences for the abolition of exemptions and zero-ratings. 'Take a running jump!' was the British response to the Commission in 1973, to other member-states in 1974 and 1975 and to the Commission again in 1982.[58] Others in the Community may interpret that

Article 28 of the Sixth Directive commits the United Kingdom to a Continental fiscal philosophy and to the eventual adjustment of the British VAT toward greater conformity with others in the EC. However, there is little evidence in British attitudes or behavior to substantiate this interpretation. The United Kingdom is committed to continuing participation in the Common Market; the Referendum underlined this commitment, and the general election of 1983 probably settled the question of British membership for a long time to come. But London's commitment to European integration, or the political will to deepen and broaden collaboration and harmonization, remains ambiguous. To the extent that the experience of the Sixth Directive reveals something about more general British attitudes, it would seem that the British intend to accept only as much of Europe as suits their immediate interests.

But again, in a broader context, British attitudes and behavior during the negotiation of the Sixth Directive may also tell us something about the evolution of the European Community during the last decade. The British pragmatic approach to the EEC is not without precedent. Gaullist France behaved in the same manner, particularly between 1964 and 1966, but French chauvinism failed to deeply infect other member-countries or to significantly dampen European idealism. However, since the mid-1970s, with the series of jolts to the world economy and the new emergence of economic nationalism, European cooperation has become increasingly cautious and constrained. Within the EEC, 'Community spirit' has become something of an anachronism and a thoroughly pragmatic ethos has come to prevail. Pursuits after short-term interests, national and Community, have come to obscure considerations about longer-term goals, and national cost-benefit thinking tends now to strictly inform members' positions on almost all issues. In this perspective, Britain's unyielding obstinacy, its outspoken defenses of national interest and its irreverence about things 'communautaire' may simply have been early manifestations of a new Community political mood. As travellers attest these days, there is a great deal of English spoken in Brussels.

Notes

1. Commission of the European Communities, 'New Proposal on the Harmonization of the VAT,' *Bulletin of the European Communities*, Supplement 11/73, Brussels, 1973; See also, Pierre Guieu, 'La proposition de la sixième directive du Conseil en matière de TVA —Assiette uniforme,' *Intertax*, No. 4/5 (January 1974), pp. 97–102.
2. Second VAT Directive, Article 17; See also, Chapter 4, p. 80.
3. Nigel Fisher, *Iain Macleod*, London, André Deutsch Ltd., 1973, pp. 284–307.
4. David Butler and Michael Pinto-Duschinsky, *The British General Election of 1970*, London, Macmillan, 1971, pp. 62–75; Conservative Research Department, 'Verbatim Report of an Economic Seminar,' *Old Queen Street Paper No. 2*, London, Conservative Party Central Office, 1967.
5. Conservative Research Department, 'Britain's Taxes: Some International Comparisons,' *Old Queen Street Paper No. 3*, London, Conservative Party Central Office, 25 September 1967; Maclennan, *et al.*, op cit. (see p. 61, n. 5), pp. 203–17; Douglas Dosser and S.S. Han, *Taxes in the EEC and Britain*, London, PEP/Chatham House, 1968, *passim*.
6. Schmölders, op. cit. (see p. 61, n. 7), p. 25. For a more elaborate description of the Purchase Tax, see *National Institute Economic Review*, No. 60 (May 1972), pp. 16–21.
7. David Butler and Michael Pinto-Duschinsky, op. cit., p. 73.
8. Ibid., pp. 73–4.
9. Interview, London, 18 November 1982.
10. Butler and Pinto-Duschinsky, op. cit., p. 73; Nigel Fisher, op. cit., p. 289.
11. *Report of the Committee on Turnover Taxation* (Richardson Report), Cmnd. 2300, HMSO, 1964, p. 124.
12. *The Times*, London, 23 January 1970.
13. Butler and Pinto-Duschinsky, op. cit., p. 66; S. Brittan, 'Thoughts on the Conservative Opposition,' *Political Quarterly* (April/June 1968), pp. 145–55; J. Bruce-Gardyne, MP, 'The Strains of Opposition,' *Spectator*, 13 September 1968.
14. Iain Macleod, 'Taxation: Planning for Office,' *The Banker*, Vol. 119, No. 518 (April 1969), pp. 306–12.
15. Interview, London, 19 November 1982.
16. *The Times*, London, 10 October 1969.
17. Iain Macleod, who would have led the fiscal reform effort as Chancellor of the Exchequer, died in July 1970. Anthony Barber was recalled from Brussels, where he was leading the British nego-

tiators in the EC Accession talks, and was appointed Chancellor. Terrence Higgins was the Treasury Secretary directly responsible for the legislative fate of the VAT.

18. *Value-added Tax* (Green Paper), Cmnd 4621, London, HMSO, 1971.

19. Ibid., p. 3.

20. *Value-added Tax* (White Paper), Cmnd 4929, London, HMSO, 1972.

21. Ibid., pp. 1–57; *The Times*, London, 22 March 1972.

22. Technically, this was not the case since the abolition of the SET and the Purchase Tax in conjunction with the introduction of the VAT actually lowered some prices. This, however, was not widely perceived among the British public.

23. Interview, 16 November 1982.

24. Disquiet among the trade associations and interest groups was widely reported in the British press. See, for example, *The Times*, London, 21 May 1971, 19 June 1971, 3 August 1971, 6 October 1971, 1 November 1971, 10 December 1971 and 15 June 1972.

25. *The Times*, London, 20 July 1972; Interview, London, 12 November 1982; Michael Pinto-Duschinsky, 'Central Office and "Power" in the Conservative Party,' *Political Studies*, Vol. 20, No. 1 (1972), pp. 1–16.

26. Interview, London, 12 November 1982.

27. *The Times*, London, 1 June 1971, 17 May 1972, 4 December 1972.

28. *The Times*, London, 17 May 1972.

29. *The Times*, London, 4 December 1972.

30. *The Times*, London, 9 November 1972.

31. *The Times*, London, 3 April 1971.

32. *The Times*, London, 10 May 1972.

33. *The Times*, London, 10 May 1972.

34. *The Times*, London, 29 March 1973.

35. Letter to *The Times*, London, by R. M. Rouse, 18 April 1972.

36. Interviews in London in November 1982 confirmed this.

37. The Labour leadership had decided by 1972 that they would consult the British people directly about staying in the EEC, but they had not yet decided upon a referendum.

38. Anthony King, *Britain Says Yes: The 1975 Referendum on the Common Market*, Washington, American Enterprise Institute for Public Policy Research, 1977, pp. 20 and 27.

39. Anthony King, op. cit., p. 71; *The Times*, London, 2 June 1975.

40. *The Times*, London, 1 June 1971; 26 August 1971.

41. Interview, London, 16 November 1982.

42. *The Times*, London, 31 May 1973.
43. Pierre Guieu, 'Le système européen de taxe sur valeur adjoutée,' *Droit Des Affaires Dans Les Pays Du Marché Commun*, France, Editions Jupiter, 1979, Tome VII, Partie II, p. 60/6; Commission of the European Communities, 'New Proposal on the Harmonization of VAT,' op. cit., *passim*.
44. This point was made dramatically by an anti-Market MP during the Referendum campaign who commented that unless the Government was prepared to 'spew out vetoes like machine gun bullets, thus bringing into question its good faith toward the harmonization of taxes, the United Kingdom would be compelled to have a much more complex system of Value-Added Tax under EEC rules.' *The Times*, London, 2 June 1975.
45. Interviews, London, 12 November 1982 and 15 November 1982.
46. Interview, London, 12 November 1982.
47. Interview, London, 15 November 1982.
48. Anthony King, op. cit., p. 71; *Labour's Programme for Britain*, London, Labour Party, 1973, p. 41ff; *The Times*, London, 6 July 1972.
49. The British were not alone in their resistance. Ireland and Denmark were also defending zero-ratings in their VAT systems.
50. *The Economist*, 5 May 1973, p. 57; *The Economist*, 29 November 1975, pp. 45–6.
51. The German (and French) argument had merit. Those dealing in zero-rated products were permitted to deduct the VAT paid on inputs, but were not required to pay a VAT charge on sales. The costs of production were therefore subsidized.
52. Interview, Brussels, 14 April 1983.
53. The number of times that this French fiscal 'theology' was described during interviews with Brussels officials suggests Paris must have made this case often and with conviction.
54. *The Economist*, 5 May 1973, p. 57.
55. Interviews, London, 15 November 1982; Brussels, 14 April 1983.
56. *Sixth Council Directive of 17 May 1977 On the Harmonization of the Laws of Member States Relating to Turnover Taxes*, 'Common System of Value Added Tax: Uniform Basis of Assessment,' Cmnd. (75) 950 final.
57. European Parliament, *Working Documents*, 1975–1976, Document 110/75.
58. Commission of the European Communities, *Report from the Commission to the Council on the Transitional Provisions Applicable Under the Common System of VAT*, Cmnd (82), 885 final, pp. 2–5.

7

Lessons in international cooperation

Fiscal harmonization in the European Communities is stalled once again. Any movement toward abolishing fiscal frontiers by standardizing the rates of the Value Added Tax Community-wide must await the full application of the Sixth Directive. This means that before any further progress can be made, those states still pursuing the 'transitional' practices allowed in Article 28 must adjust their VAT systems to prescribed form.[1] As Chapter 6 made clear, for the British (and perhaps the Irish) this implies a change of will; for others, like the Greeks, an enhancement of political capacity will be required. Commission officials, however, retain their positive outlooks: while they tend to agree that 'successes have been limited' in the field of tax harmonization, they also remain convinced that 'eventually . . . closer alignment . . . will be necessary.'[2]

Very little that has been presented in this book makes it possible to predict *how far* the European Communities are going to go toward completing fiscal harmonization in the years ahead. But, on the basis of previous analysis, a good deal can be said about *whether* the Communities are likely to move forward at all, about *how fast* they are likely to move, and about the *process or processes* that will be triggered as they face and take the next steps. While, in a strict social scientific sense this book's lessons can apply only to fiscal harmonization, further research could very well show that they are generally applicable across a range of EC issues. There is also some reason to believe that by examining the politics of fiscal harmonization in Europe we may have learned something important about international cooperation among western democracies. The purpose of this last chapter is to reflect on such lessons learned.

Some Lessons from the VAT Cases

Domestic Politics and the EC Policy Process

During the first one and a half decades of the EC's existence, the ease or difficulty involved in reaching inter-governmental agreements on policy issues was apparently only rarely determined by governments' political will. This was not because the will to cooperate was unimportant, but rather because it was generally present. Member-governments valued the European Community; national interests were understood to be served by membership and by the goal of creating a common market; commitments to reach agreement were taken seriously; governments wanted to cooperate. There was no evidence of failed will in three of the four cases analyzed. During their respective periods of difficulty with the VAT, neither the West German, the Dutch nor the Italian Government questioned the desirability of fiscal harmonization or indicated that they did not wish to cooperate with Community partners in working towards it. In fact, these governments repeatedly reaffirmed their commitments to the goals of fiscal harmonization even while they were temporarily blocking progress. Initial British expressions of goodwill were similar, and it was not until the Community began debating the Sixth Directive that London signalled a dampening of will by asserting that it would not fully align its VAT system with those of its Continental partners even if this threatened the future course of Community affairs. Yet, in context, and by comparison, the British attitude was unusual. Up to this point, with regard to fiscal harmonization at least, political will generally had not been the problem.

Instead, the course of Community policy-making tended to be more frequently influenced by governments' political capacities to cooperate internationally, or, in other words, by their abilities or inabilities to act accommodatingly toward each other and the European Commission. The case studies showed that political capacity was largely determined by balances of domestic political support and opposition regarding various national stances in Brussels. When, for reasons of their own, the preponderance of parties, forces and factions within countries could accept and support doing things 'Brussels' way,' political capacities of member-governments were enhanced, and they were freed to join in Community consensus, or even to lead in promoting it. This was clearly the case for Germany with regard to fiscal harmonization after 1964.

The case studies also showed, however, that there was in national politics a more general bias against doing things 'Brussels' way.' This was because accepting Community-wide harmonization usually required adjustment or change within member-states. Comfortable, previously-bargained status quos were thereby upset; vested interests were threatened; all manner of defensive political action ensued, and mounting opposition reduced governments' political capacities. Recall in the cases, for example, how national factions repeatedly rallied around previously existing turn-over taxes with which they were familiar, and under which they were often favored (or exempted). By contrast, they feared the untried VAT, expected penalties under it and therefore opposed it. In this way, Community issues injected into national affairs tended to be quickly and often intensely politicized. Their playing out in domestic political arenas sometimes threatened the stability of governments, as in the Italian case, or at least aroused the political sensitivities and anxieties of elected officials, as in Germany, the Netherlands and the United Kingdom. This usually constrained national governments to behave cautiously in Brussels, and prompted them to avoid international commitments that would exacerbate the domestic pressures upon them. Contests in domestic politics, then, repeatedly affected member-governments' political capacities to cooperate internationally and this crucially affected the character of the EC policy process.

Delay in Brussels was the most readily apparent result of the different governments' domestic political incapacities. When domestic pressures forced certain governments into contrary stances, productive policy-making halted in Brussels. As long as the problems causing the delays were in domestic arenas, there was very little that the Commission or other member-governments could do directly to force closure in Brussels. Unanimity prevailed in the Council of Ministers, so that uncooperative members could not be procedurally forced to alter their positions. Neither did diplomatic pressures, such as those brought to bear on the Dutch, or formal enforcement procedures under the Rome Treaty, as were waved before Italy, appear to have much bearing. For the recalcitrant governments, the domestic political costs of yielding in Brussels, measured in terms of tranquility, stability and continuity in office at home, perceptibly outweighed any sanctions that the EEC could impose. They therefore stood firm, and often alone, until domestic pressures diminished, and Community decisions were accordingly postponed.

As a result of the close relationship between domestic political constraints in member-states and the pace of policy-making in Brussels, Community outcomes in the form of decisions, directives, and recommendations, almost invariably called upon member-governments to initiate actions that they could live with politically at home. Obviously, no government would permit any measure to pass through the Council of Ministers that would be likely to arouse consequential domestic opposition. When this apparently happened in the Italian case after the adoption of the Second VAT Directive, analysis showed it to be something of a rule-proving exception. Rome had simply miscalculated politically. Otherwise, the VAT Directives were negotiated and renegotiated until all that might offend any strong political interest in any member-state had been removed. But, in negotiating EC fiscal policies with an eye to their political situations, most member-governments sought not only to avoid adverse repercussions, but also to enhance their standing in home arenas. Their object was to 'bring something home from Brussels' that would either reward their domestic supporters, add new supporters, or undermine their opponents.[3] The West German Government, for example, wanted, and got, a Community VAT Directive that could be used in Bonn to pry at the opponents of German tax reform; Dutch Prime Minister Zijlstra wanted, and got, dispensations in the Second Directive that would permit him to rebuild his standing with his Ministry of Finance; the British Government wanted, and got, the opportunity to appear the staunch defender of

English fiscal tradition. Needless to say, narrow political self-interests are not the only ends that governments play for in Brussels. But they are vitally important, as each of the four case studies rather dramatically illustrated. Any analysis of the EC policy process that did not take account of them would be sadly lacking.

The Politics of Mutual Responsiveness

What was also remarkable about the EC policy process as revealed in the case studies was that member-governments easily recognized each others' political incapacities, and usually tolerated them. The Commission too was generally well aware of what was happening politically within member-states, and it most often accurately understood the domestic causes of besieged governments' uncooperative stances. An unwritten guideline in such situations was 'don't rock the political boat in member-countries with domestic problems.' As a rule, member-governments, sensitive to each others' political situations, acted to avoid aggravating tensions within other countries, and the Commission acted similarly. This sometimes meant doing nothing at all, since anything that looked to be outside interference in a country's domestic affairs could easily amplify pressures upon its government. In the Italian case, for example, the Commission and the Council backed away from sanctions against Italy in the autumn of 1970 when it became apparent that these would likely contribute to the anti-VAT *furor* in Rome. Similarly, in the British case, Commissioner Simonet withdrew his call for the removal of zero-rates from the UK's new VAT after he visited London in the early summer of 1973. It might be reasonably assumed in this instance that during his stay in England the Commissioner was reminded about the sanctity of certain tax exemptions in British fiscal tradition.[4]

More often, however, Council partners and the Brussels authorities looked for ways to help domestically-blocked governments resolve their problems so that the EC policy process could be moved along. As experience taught that agreement was unlikely to be gained by forcing governments into political corners at home, the alternative was to try to help partners out of domestically difficult spots. Such help frequently took the form of 'giving them something to take home from Brussels,' or as one European journalist phrased it, 'letting them have some pelts to hang from the belt.' In the German case, for example, the Commission knew that the Bonn Government needed a VAT proposal in 1964 that looked as much as possible like the VAT Bill then before the Bundestag. Authorities in Brussels also understood the importance of this match in the West German political context, and they made efforts to meet the Erhard Government's needs. Similarly, in the Dutch case, Council partners in the winter of 1967 recognized that Prime Minister Zijlstra needed to pacify his disgruntled Finance Ministry, and Article 17 of the Second VAT Directive was written and adopted with this in mind. Almost in the same way, Article 28 of the Sixth VAT Directive gave the British Government something politically helpful to take back home.

In the VAT cases, such acts of responsiveness were primarily pragmatic. That is, they were calculated and taken to help break political logjams within blocked countries so that Community outcomes could be attained which cooperating member-governments and the Commission deemed to be in their respective self-interests. Yet, there was also a certain amount of empathy in such complementary behavior, especially on the part of Council partners. At one time or another they were all likely to find themselves caught between domestic constraints and EC imperatives, and as they all lived in political glasshouses they tended to be rather cautious about throwing stones.

But there were also limits to complementary behavior. For one thing, it was frequently unproductive to engage in it very openly since this could cause domestic problems for the governments that were acting responsively. When Italy asked to postpone its VAT, for example, export industries in Gemany and the Netherlands pressed their respective governments to go hard on the Italians and to sanction them for refusing to abolish the IGE on time. For domestic reasons, therefore, the German and Dutch governments had at least to make a show of encouraging the Commission to come down on Rome, and the Commission in turn also had to show its rigor in order to preserve credibility as the enforcer of the

Community's rules. Behind the scenes, the Italian Government was assured that its political problems were understood, that the postponement would be allowed, that rigorous conditions would not be imposed and that talk of severe sanctions was for public consumption in other countries. Nevertheless, the public displays cancelled the effects of the quiet diplomacy because the Italian press picked up and dramatized the harsher exchanges and missed the complementary messages. Consequently, factions in Italy already opposed to the VAT were told in the press that the EC Council and Commission were badgering their Government. They redoubled their opposition and further incapacitated the Rome Government.

But, despite occasional backfires, moves reflecting mutual political sensitivity and responsiveness abetted the EC policy process during the entire period covered by the four VAT case studies. The mutual appreciation of the domestic political causes of governments' uncooperativeness minimized both unproductive rhetoric and counterproductive behavior in Community councils. Such qualities as mutual political understanding, sensitivity and responsiveness are extraordinary in International Relations, and, when present, they indicate a level of affinity among governments that is a good deal higher than that ordinarily attained in state-to-state affairs.[5] This 'closeness' as exhibited in the case studies repeatedly catalyzed consensus.

Politics, Harmonization and Integration

Needless to say, framing Community directives and standardizing national laws to comply with their prescriptions, or what in Brussels is called 'harmonization,' is not all that is meant by European Integration. Among other things, the process of international integration involves institution-building, political-structural change, political-cultural change and social assimilation among peoples.[6] At the practical level, however, promoting transnational harmonization accounts for a substantial proportion of what the European Communities actually do. Furthermore, the cumulative effects of these day-to-day activities have rendered European national frontiers less and less relevant to economic intercourse and policy. As a result of the EC's common policies and the alignments in national rules and practices that these have impelled, the European Communities are becoming a *common market*, and, under the Rome Treaty this, at least minimally, is what European Integration was supposed to produce. To the extent that a standardized tax regime has been established, fiscal harmonization has contributed to completing the Common Market and therefore in a modest way also to European Integration.

Although the main concerns of this book have been with the problems and pitfalls along the way to fiscal harmonization, this should not cloud the fact that integrative progress was being made in the fiscal field right up to the mid-1970s. A Community turnover tax was created and implemented as prescribed by the Rome Treaty, a common base of assessment was agreed, and Brussels authorities began collecting their own resources. With regard to turnover taxes, the Communities are technically two-thirds of the way toward attaining their goal of abolishing fiscal frontiers, though politically they are probably much more distant. Nevertheless, there has been progress.

The case studies indicate that what integrative progress there has been in fiscal affairs followed in notable measure from the fact that the European Commission and Council of Ministers were able to accommodate disruptions in Community policy-making caused by adverse domestic political developments within member-states. It has already been explained that such abilities were enhanced by a high degree of mutual sensitivity and responsiveness among Community actors. But there were several other factors that also helped the Community deal successfully with politically-constrained member-governments, and thereby contributed to the cumulative integration of the turnover tax system. These factors were of a political-psychological nature for the most part, and had to do with attitudes and expectations that participants brought to the EC policy process.

First, unanimity was the expected and accepted decision-making norm. National vetoes in the Council of Ministers, either threatened or actually cast, were functional to the policy process because they allowed governments a most

effective means of stopping Community action when this had
to be done for domestic political reasons. Thus, governments
seeking time to rally domestic support or overcome opposition regarding Brussels' requests could almost always gain the
time they needed by stopping the European policy process.
Were it not for the veto, impatience or frustration in the
Council of Ministers might at times have made temptations
to ride roughshod over recalcitrant governments irresistible.
Such power plays probably would not have brought
compliance from dissenting governments because they
usually could not change their domestic situations or therefore alter their political incapacities. What is more likely is
that they would have alienated these governments by forcing
them into political quandaries. This might have dampened
their will to cooperate further and thus caused damage to the
Community.

Second, member-governments and the Commission
expected and accepted that Community policy-making
would proceed at a pace determined by the slowest-moving
member-government. Patience was apparently a part of the
Community ethos. Participants experienced in the EC's
intricate multilateral diplomacy and attuned to patterns of
political reverberation, hardly ever expected that things
would move either smoothly or rapidly. Delays caused by
domestic blockages were therefore perceived as routine
occurrences rather than crisis-provoking incidents. They
were, moreover, looked upon as *postponements* only and
constantly referred to as such, as if to emphasize their anticipated transitory nature. Impatience was sometimes displayed
by the Commission or in the Council, as in the Dutch case,
but largely for the tactical purpose of keeping stalled governments aware that their domestic problems needed to be
resolved. Pressures of time, however, were not otherwise
widely acknowledged. Anything could be postponed as long
as ultimate goals were not abandoned. This did little to
enhance the efficiency of the EC policy process. But it added
greatly to its durability, and, in the field of fiscal harmonization at least, tolerance for slow movement interspersed with
delays definitely contributed to the integrative successes
achieved.

Third, member-governments and the Commission also expected and accepted that the ambitiousness of any agreed integrative step would be determined by the most constrained government. Outcomes then would be of the lowest-denominator variety, and these were acceptable, even to the Commission, as long as they represented steps toward ultimate Community goals. The VAT cases showed that participants in the EC policy process were not attuned to taking giant integrative leaps, but that they rather looked for small, sometimes barely perceptible, cumulative steps. Agreements about principles, as when the Six accepted that the harmonized turnover tax would be of the value added variety, or when the Nine later agreed that exemptions and zero-ratings must eventually be eliminated, were considered to be integrative steps in and of themselves even though they impelled no immediate changes in behavior. Indeed, no one expected that national behavior could be quickly changed. In the same way, what appeared to be major movements, as when the Second and Sixth VAT Directives were adopted, were actually only modest steps since acceptability rested upon the inclusion of numerous escape clauses and long transitional periods. This was as it had to be because different governments, differentially constrained domestically, were able to go to different harmonizing lengths at different points in time. And, they were rarely forced farther than they believed they could safely go in light of their domestic situations. Here again, the Italian case was the exception that proved the rule, and the crisis that erupted in Italy affirmed the rule's importance.

Paradoxically then, what many have criticized as weaknesses in the EC policy process—i.e., its unanimity requirements, tediousness, and lowest-denominator results—turn out upon analysis to be sources of considerable strength. These qualities, implanted into participants' expectations, and thus transformed into elements of the Community ethos, injected flexibility and durability into the EC policy process. They offered hedges against crises and complete breakdowns at times when national governments were domestically constrained to be internationally uncooperative. Yet, it must be underlined that integrative results tended to follow from such allowances for unanimity, slow movement and incremental outcomes only in the context of a continuing political will to reach ultimate goals. If participants abandoned their commitments to create an ever more integrated system, vetoes could become devices to sabotage collective aims instead of means to buy time to build consensus. Similarly, delays could come to signal intransigence rather than adjustments in response to political reverberation, and lowest-denominator outcomes could drop completely out of the 'integrative' range.

Up to the time of the debates over the Sixth Directive, there was little in the fiscal harmonization experience to suggest that it would not eventually progress all the way to the abolition of fiscal frontiers. The policy process was moving tediously; delays were frequent and sometimes long-lasting; integrative steps were small ones and depended upon unanimity. But political will remained constant, and this meant that the domestic contests that were causing the painfully slow movement were being resolved in ways that finally permitted constrained governments to cooperate in Community councils. As long as this pattern persisted the best prediction would be that harmonization would continue to creep forward. However, the tenor of the Sixth Directive debates, and particularly British performance, raised questions about continuing political will and therefore about whether further integrative progress will be made. The EC policy process is able to accommodate disruptions caused by domestically-constrained governments, but only if the governments are themselves willing to resolve domestic problems in ways that will later permit them to rejoin in Community consensus. By the mid-1970s some governments were beginning to exhibit reluctance in this regard. Not only does this bode poorly for fiscal harmonization, but if it reflects generally changing national attitudes about cooperation in the EC it could infect a range of issues.

International Cooperation Among Western Democracies

As noted in Chapter 1, the purpose of this study has been not only to learn about the European Communities, but also to learn from them. For some time now it has been fashion-able among students of international affairs to discount the accomplishments of the European Communities. We are told that European Integration has failed: there will be no United States of Europe. International economic problems in the 1970s and 1980s, it is said, have torn at the fabric of the Common Market and forced EC governments onto divergent courses. This has rendered meaningful cooperation difficult and pushed supranationality beyond reach. In fact, some observers sense that there has been a resurgence of economic nationalism within Western Europe, and they fear that disintegration may have begun. It is also held that the 'European Spirit,' or whatever remains of it, is the faith of an older generation, the majority of whom are no longer politi-cally active, and those still at work are not very influential.

Academic attitudes toward the EC today are equally dis-missive. Compared with the intense theoretical and practical interest in Community affairs displayed by academics in the 1960s, analytical attention is presently meager. The pro-fessors tell us that European Integration is not going any-where. So why study it? Practically speaking, what is to be learned from a failed idealism, a set of malfunctioning insti-tutions, a policy regime that very few are happy with, or a bureaucracy that produces mostly paper? Theoretically, what is to be gained from refurbishing integration theory, if there are no cases of integration?

The critics of the European Communities are wrong in just about every one of their assertions, except perhaps in their contention that a United States of Europe is unlikely.[7] However, the purpose of this study has not been to rebut Europe's present-day detractors. It has rather been to see what can be learned about international cooperation among western industrial democracies from a set of intra-European experiences that occurred at times when most would agree that the European Communities were running rather well. What makes the search for lessons in these European cases both fascinating and challenging is that the episodes are specimens of a historically rare phenomenon—*extended, productive, cumulatively broadening and deepening, multi-lateral, international cooperation*! Contemporary International

Relations would undoubtedly benefit greatly if this phenomenon were not so rare. It therefore behoves us to understand it as thoroughly as possible in the hope that new
knowledge might contribute to more promising practice.
Thus, whatever its current problems and future development,
the EEC remains a laboratory for the study of creative international collaboration, and this book has been a modest
puttering about in the laboratory.

Democracy and International Collaboration

One commonsense lesson of the European experiences
examined in this book is that it is extremely difficult for
democratic countries to cooperate with one another even
when their governments and peoples genuinely want to. The
VAT cases showed that pursuing a common, patently reasonable and relatively modest goal turned out to be an ordeal of
major proportions for most of the EC governments involved.
This happened largely because the EC member-states are
pluralistic industrial democracies.[8] Democratic government
in the West is by historical and contemporary comparison far
and away the most humanistically benign form of government ever devised. It is highly valued and must be protected
and preserved. But the political workings of pluralist
democracy can create problems in the pursuit of foreign
relations. Governments in democratic countries remain
stable, and in office, as long as they retain the support of
electoral majorities, and since they tend to be either coalition
or mass party regimes, they must draw their support from
rather wide cross-sections of their societies. Notably, they
cannot afford to alienate very many groups, factions, sectors
or classes without directly jeopardizing their tenure in office.
Governments must therefore govern by distributing material
and symbolic rewards as widely as possible in their societies
or by protecting as much of society as possible from penalty.
In this sense all of the Western governments are weak inasmuch as they can be readily undermined electorally. They are
also constrained because their range of policy options is
delimited by the degrees of electoral alienation they can
tolerate and still hope to stay in office. A distinguishing
characteristic of international relations among pluralist

democracies then is that they are relations among rather fragile governments who must constantly be concerned about their electoral bases. This was amply clear from the European case studies.

The Western democracies are also welfare states and national electorates have therefore come to expect that their governments will see to their economic well-being.[9] Politics in welfare states are mostly about economic issues, and governments most frequently gain or lose office on the basis of their economic promises or performances. Economic questions then become quickly and highly politicized: they provoke controversy and contests among interests and factions that directly affect governments' electoral fates and fortunes. Since economic issues tend to be crisis-provoking in Western welfare state politics, governments tend to be extraordinarily sensitive, cautious and electorally conscious about them. Another distinguishing feature of international relations among Western democracies, therefore, is that when economic issues are under discussion, as they are most of the time, governments will be as much concerned with domestic politicization as with diplomatic outcomes. Domestic politicization then will directly affect diplomatic results. This too was apparent in the European cases.

Thus, efforts at international cooperation among Western industrial democracies, particularly on economic questions, usually occur in highly-charged political environments. In these contexts domestic policy cannot be easily or neatly separated from foreign policy and vice versa. But when there are contradictions or conflicts, domestic political concerns take precedence over international consensus.[10] Furthermore, during efforts at international cooperation among industrial democracies, at least three sets of interests tend to be pursued simultaneously, 'national' interests, 'governments'' interests, and 'international' or 'collaborative' interests. The first have to do with the preferences or goals of the electoral coalitions that support particular governments ·or, more immediately, with what these groups can be persuaded to accept as government policy. Second are governments' own objectives in maintaining office by rewarding their supporters and undermining their opponents, as well as their objectives in forging and maintaining productive relationships with other governments. Third are the anticipated benefits for economy and society from collective international action. It is to seek these that countries try to cooperate in the first place. As long as 'interests' in all senses coincide or converge, states are able to cooperate to their mutual benefit. But when 'interests' conflict, democratic governments almost always give precedence to their own political interests by catering to 'national' interests as here defined. Productive relations with neighbors and collective international goals are thus either de-emphasized or transferred to wish lists for the future.

The Elements of Successful International Collaboration

The second commonsense lesson from European experience is that while achieving productive cooperation among industrial democracies is extremely difficult, it is far from impossible and a good deal can be done to facilitate it. Many of the necessary conditions for successful international cooperation have already been discussed with specific regard to the VAT cases. What remains is to summarize these in more general terms.

At least two of the conditions necessary for international cooperation among industrial democracies concern the governments of such countries taken individually. Each government must possess the *will* and the *capacity* to enter into collaborative international undertakings. 'Will' follows from governing elites' convictions that the goals of planned collective action are in their medium and long-term interest, and that collective action is the most beneficial or least costly way to attain national goals. Political will, as it relates to international cooperation, also entails a commitment to join in collective goal-pursuits whenever possible, and, when this is impossible, to take all feasible steps to make it so. As noted earlier, 'will' was not dwelt upon in most of the VAT case analyses, because it was present in the European setting and could therefore be taken as a given. But it must be underlined and forcefully stressed that there can be no international cooperation unless governments want it, and they are most likely to want it when perceived collective and self interests coincide or converge. The presence versus the absence of the political will to cooperate, for example, sharply distinguishes the customary diplomacy of the European Communities from what generally takes place in the political organs of the United Nations.[11]

It is hardly necessary to reiterate the importance of political capacity. This is largely what this book has been about. To want to cooperate internationally is not sufficient. Governments must also be able to cooperate, and in international relations among democratic countries this means that domestic political conditions must be right. Unfortunately they seldom are, and this accounts in no small measure for the comparative rarity of extended cooperation among democratic countries. Moreover, because of politicization, Western governments' capacities to cooperate tend to be most constrained in economic issue areas, where, paradoxically, the imperatives of their interdependence render collaboration most necessary and discord most costly. As long as the will to cooperate remains constant, however, the European cases demonstrated that governments can enhance their capacities to cooperate by mobilizing domestic support for and overcoming opposition to internationally collaborative behavior. This usually takes time, and it takes resources since governing Western democracies is largely a matter of exchanging rewards and sidepayments for support.

To facilitate international cooperation, diplomatic interactions must have the effect of fortifying the political wills and enhancing the political capacities of individual governments. European experience teaches that leadership, management, sensitivity, responsiveness and ethos are necessary to achieve these effects.

Leadership. Collective action on a transnational issue is never initiated spontaneously. At least one government must want a collective outcome, badly enough, usually for domestic reasons, to take the lead in rallying and mobilizing partners. Otherwise, governments potentially involved in the collaborative undertaking, but who assign lower priority to its outcome, could well choose not to raise the issue lest it be politicized in their countries. Cooperation would thus remain a 'good idea' that no one wished to risk trying, as was the case with European fiscal harmonization where the notion got almost nowhere until the German Government began to promote it. To be effective, however, leadership toward international collaboration must be able to invoke symbolism that calls attention to previous collective expressions of political will. Treaty commitments, declarations at past Summits and similar solemnized pronouncements provide such symbols. By using them, the leader is able to encourage partners to 'get cracking on something that we all agreed we wanted to accomplish,' and thus start governments working to improve their political capacities to cooperate. Revealingly, attempts to exercise leadership on the basis of power or 'clout' seldom have desired effects.

Management. European experience suggests that pursuing issues through to productive, collective outcomes is usually an exceedingly lengthy process. Therefore, once international cooperation is initiated, it generally has to be kept going for an extended period of time in order to yield desired results. Because of this it is constantly necessary to combat governments' tendencies toward short-term thinking, their fickleness in attention and priority, and their propensities to frequently change personnel. Moreover, since elections periodically intervene, it is not unusual for governments to change completely in the course of particular international negotiations, thus creating disruptions and discontinuities that have to be contained. On the other hand, governments will sometimes simply tire of dealing with a complex or apparently intractable issue and choose to move to other matters, or, more frequently, they may begin to feel pressures from domestic opposition and attempt to back away from cooperation. If collective ends are to be attained, therefore, governments must be kept involved in the collaborative process and committed to its goals even as these become increasingly blurred and distant.

International 'management' means lending organization and continuity to extended inter-governmental negotiations. Initiating governments might also be diplomatic managers. But they are prone to the same kinds of pressures, short-term thinking and fickleness as their partners and therefore often prove to be unreliable over the long haul. European experience shows that international secretariats are better suited to the management assignment, largely because they go about it with single-minded, unremitting purpose. Furthermore, their institutional self-interests are bound to successful inter-governmental cooperation. In the EC the Commission and the Council Secretariat manage negotiations during the European policy process. The political effects of their activities are seldom decisive because the final substance of inter-governmental agreements almost always emerges from bargains among ministers. Yet, the institutional managers' significance is less in the substance they contribute than in the dynamism they supply. Their technical work clears away problems of information so that what governments negotiate are not matters of statistics or legal reference but differences of political interest. But even more importantly, the international secretariats keep the issues constantly before the national governments by organizing and reporting upon studies, by setting timetables and agendas, by calling and chairing repeated meetings, by drafting agreements and by proposing compromises. The bureaucrats keep the diplomats talking: when negotiations stall at higher levels, they call meetings at lower levels; when matters prove intractable at lower levels, they move discussions to higher ones. When deadlocks develop, they propose ways out. As each step toward agreement is taken, the international bureaucracy is already proposing the next. The managers drive the motors of international cooperation, and European experience shows them to be absolutely necessary in the mediation of collaboration among Western democracies.

Sensitivity and Responsiveness. In his perceptive study of Anglo-American relations, Richard E. Neustadt illustrated some of the diplomatically devastating results of governments' mutual political insensitivities and non-responsiveness.[12] What Neustadt found was surprising, as we might have expected that Britons and Americans—common heritage, 'special relationship' and all—should have understood one another's domestic politics better. However, his findings were not at all extraordinary in the context of customary International Relations, where, as rule, governments do not understand each others' domestic affairs very well and they frequently blunder diplomatically precisely because of this. This is characteristically the case when at least one of the governments involved is a Western democracy where, for all of the reasons cited earlier, domestic and foreign policy-making are closely intertwined. When both or all of the interacting states are democracies problems of mutual political misunderstanding can be greatly compounded.

European experience shows that successful international cooperation among Western democracies requires rather high degrees of mutual political familiarity that can be diplomatically translated into mutual sensitivity and responsiveness. This point was made earlier in this chapter and need not be elaborated again. Yet, it cannot be stressed too strongly that during most of the period of this study intra-EEC diplomacy was qualitatively different from traditional international relations. Not only were participating governments and international authorities acutely and accurately aware of political situations within all member-countries, but they repeatedly acted to minimize or circumvent the disruptive impacts of these situations on international collaboration. To a considerable extent, then, the diplomacy of international cooperation must be a process of mutual domestic political accommodation.

Ethos. European experience also suggests that collaborative diplomacy is conditioned by informal codes of conduct, tacit understandings among participants, or, in the vocabulary of the Theory of International Regimes, sets of 'rules of the game.'[13] These have the effect of sometimes avoiding conflict, dampening it when it occurs, and establishing frameworks of expectations within which it can be satisfactorily resolved. Only further research can determine which of the norms observed in the European cases were EC-specific and which are broader elements of the ethos of international cooperation. It would appear, however, that successful international cooperation is founded at least in the shared understanding that:

— diplomatic outcomes must reward all participating governments, or at least penalize none;

—diplomatic outcomes must buttress the domestic political
standings of all participating governments, or at least
jeopardize none;

—diplomatic moves that aggravate domestic political difficulties for other governments are inappropriate;

—diplomatic moves that ameliorate domestic political
difficulties for other governments are expected;

—all decisions and agreements must be concluded unanimously, and time and terms must be allowed so that
unanimity can evolve.

It almost goes without saying that most of these norms
are not commonly observed in most contemporary diplomatic forums, Western or otherwise, and they are not even
always adhered to in intra-EEC relations. They are the ethos
of an intelligent, sensitive, subtle, moderate and patient
diplomacy, that in practice is the obverse of the zero-sum
gamesmanship of traditional power politics. This would
appear to be the only kind of diplomacy that permits international cooperation among democracies to continue and
succeed.

Notes

1. The Greek Government has yet to introduce a VAT.
2. Commission of the European Communities, *Bulletin of the European Communities*, Supplement 1/80, 'Report on the Scope for
   Convergence of Tax Systems in the Community,' Brussels, EEC,
   March, 1980, pp. 7 and 8.
3. Peter Busch and Donald Puchala, 'Interests, Influence and Integration: Political Structure in the European Communities,' *Comparative Political Studies*, Vol. 9, No. 3 (October, 1976), pp. 235–
   53.
4. *The Economist*, 5 May 1973, pp. 57–8.
5. Karl W. Deustch, *et al.*, *Political Community and the North
   Atlantic Area*, Princeton, N.J., Princeton University Press, 1957,
   pp. 129–33; Bruce M. Russett, *Community and Contention:
   Britain and America in the Twentieth Century*, Cambridge, Mass.,
   MIT Press, 1963, pp. 26–33; 144–61.

6. Ernst B. Haas, *The Uniting of Europe*, Stanford, Stanford University Press, 1958, pp. 3–59; Karl W. Deutsch, *Political Community at the International Level*, Garden City, N.Y., Doubleday & Co., 1954, *passim.*; Ernst B. Haas and Philippe C. Schmitter, 'Economics and Differential Patterns of Political Integration: Projections about Unity in Latin America,' *International Organization*, Vol. 18, No. 4 (Autumn 1964), pp. 705–37.

7. Glenda G. Rosenthal and Donald J. Puchala, 'Decisional Systems, Adaptiveness and European Decision-Making,' *The Annals of the American Academy of Political and Social Science*, Vol. 440, November, 1978, pp. 54–65.

8. For imaginative theoretical treatment of international relations among democratic governments, see Peter J. Katzenstein, 'International Relations and Domestic Structures: Foreign Economic Policies of Advanced Industrial States,' *International Organization*, Vol. 30, No. 1 (Winter 1976), pp. 1–46.

9. Gunnar Myrdal, *Beyond the Welfare State*, New York, Bantam Books, 1967, pp. 72–87.

10. Edward Morse, *Modernization and the Transformation of International Relations*, New York, The Free Press, 1976, pp. 77–113.

11. Daniel Patrick Moynihan, *A Dangerous Place*, New York, Berkeley Books, 1980, *passim.*

12. Richard E. Neustadt, *Alliance Politics*, New York, Columbia University Press, 1970, *passim.*

13. Stephen D. Krasner, (ed.), *International Regimes*, Ithaca and London, Cornell University Press, 1983, pp. 1–22 *et passim.*

Index